God's Grand Design

Booklet 2

I0137153

Blessed Mother Mary

Reveals Her Apparitions

Richard Ferguson

God's Grand Design: Blessed Mother Mary Reveals Her Apparitions
by Richard Ferguson
Copyright © 2024 by Richard Ferguson
All Rights Reserved.
ISBN: 978-1-59755-823-5

Published by: ADVANTAGE BOOKS™
                     St Johns, Florida, USA
                     www.advbookstore.com

Unless otherwise indicated, Scripture quotations taken from The Holy Bible KING JAMES VERSION (KJV), public domain.

Scriptures marked (NKJV) are taken from the Holy Bible NEW KING JAMES VERSION®. Copyright© 1982 by Thomas Nelson, Inc. Used by permission. All rights reserved.

Library of Congress Catalog Number: 2024946291

Name: Ferguson, Richard, Author
Title: *Blessed Mother Mary Reveals Her Apparitions*
             Advantage Books, 2024
ID: ISBN: 978159754213
Subjects: RELIGION: Christian Life – Inspirational

Evangeline Ferguson: Lead Contributor and Lead Editor

First Printing: November 2024
24 25 26 27 28 29 30   10 9 8 7 6 5 4 3 2 1

God Speaks To His Sacred Children about This Booklet And Its Author

"This Booklet is written for you by my special favored son. He is my sacred child, like of all of you are. But listen to what he has to say for I approve of his words in this booklet. He has worked very hard to bring you advanced truths of my creations. Richard is completely right when he describes that the spiritual realm, and the physical universe are indeed created so all of my sacred children may return to me after the rebellion of Lucifer and the fall of Adam and Eve as is described in your Christian Bible.

Listen to him with both your ears, for Richard has a unique and true understanding of things that are not available to those who believe in me by other means. I your Father in Heaven, have asked Richard to do something that I have never asked any others of my children. Listen to him for he is my Messenger, and he will help lead you back to me so we may together enjoy eternal life in a paradise that each of you can barely imagine. Yet, it is waiting for you.

Richard is one of my special children even before he was born on the earth. If you listen to what he has to say and read what he has written, that will lead you back to me without fail. I love all of you so very much from the bottom of my heart. Pray to me. Ask me questions about your lives. I will answer you. Be prepared to listen to what I have to say for it will be for your eternal goodness and salvation.

I love you, Your Loving Divine Father "

Table of Contents

INTRODUCTION 6

1: BLESSED MOTHER MARY SPEAKS 8

2: REVELATIONS NEVER HEARD BEFORE 13
  BECOMING GOD'S ANOINTED MESSENGER 16
  THE BEGINNING OF MY CHRISTIAN SPIRITUAL WARFARE 18
  THE ARRIVAL OF JESUS CHRIST AND BLESSED MOTHER MARY ..19
  WHY ME LORD? 24

3: ALL ABOUT OUR BLESSED MOTHER MARY 26
  HOW DOES BLESSED MOTHER MARY SPEAK WITH ME? 27
  THE SACRED PROCESS 28
  THE REASON MOTHER MARY SPEAKS TO ME 29
  THE BEAUTIFUL VOICE OF MOTHER MARY 31
  MOTHER MARY, THE LINK BETWEEN EARTH AND HEAVEN 35

4: FIVE APPARITIONS OF BLESSED MOTHER MARY 41
  MOTHER MARY SPEAKS TO ME ABOUT HER APPARITIONS 42
  LA SALETTE, SEPTEMBER 19, 1846. 44
  LOURDES 66
  GARABANDAL 73
  IS THE POPE FRANCIS THE ANTI-CHRIST? 89
  ZEITOUN, EGYPT 90

5: MOTHER MARY DESCRIBES FATIMA 1, 2, AND 3 97
  A DESCRIPTION OF ALL THREE FÁTIMA REVELATIONS 97
  FATIMA APPARITION 1 102
  FÁTIMA APPARITION 2 105
  FATIMA'S SECRET APPARITION 3 106
  WHAT IS A RELIABLE CATHOLIC CHRISTIAN CATECHISM. 107

6. THE REAL 3RD SECRET OF FATIMA 109

OUR BELOVED CHURCH 111

SATAN WILL PLACE HIMSELF ON THE THRONE OF PETER 112

7: THIRD SECRET OF FATIMA CONTINUES 134

WHAT WAS SAID IN THE THIRD SECRET OF FATIMA 134

FATHER MALACHI MARTIN WITH ART BELL 138

WHAT FATHER MARTIN TELLS US ABOUT THE THIRD SECRET OF

FATIMA 139

8: POPE BENEDICT 142

THE REVELATION IN FATIMA'S THIRD SECRET 142

9: MORALITY AS DEFINED BY ALMIGHTY GOD 152

10: MOTHER MARY'S CLOSING THOUGHTS 155

Introduction

This introduction contains vital information regarding how this booklet came to be and the people involved in writing it. Unless you read others of my booklets, this will be the only sacred booklet besides the Bible that is in your possession. There are especially important points that must be made in this introduction so you will be able to understand the miracle you are holding in your hand.

This booklet is a condensed version of the book titled, <u>God's Grand Design, Mother Mary Speaks Directly Her Apparitions and The End of Times</u>." The previous book mentioned here contains a lot of detailed information that would be very useful in your Christian understanding of the times we are living in and especially what is to come.

1. 100% of everything you read in this booklet is completely true and is approved by your Almighty Father in Heaven. He is with me 100% of my life and knows all my thoughts and my emotions and so on. I have been gifted enormously by Our Heavenly Father being able to speak with not only Him, but also Our Lord Jesus Christ, the Holy Spirit, which proceeds from them and Our Blessed Mother Mary. I am able to carry on conversations with the Trinity and Mother Mary. If I tell you something theological you can rest assured whatever I say is completely true. I have had a **Covenant of Truth** with Our Heavenly Father for the past 40 years or so. I will not and cannot tell a falsehood in any of its forms.

2. Your author Richard Ferguson is indeed your **Heavenly Father's Anointed Messenger.** I was chosen by Our Father for many reasons that are in the above Master Booklet and summarized here.

3. It was a momentous pleasure to have many different discussions with Our Blessed Mother Mary in the writing of this booklet. We have come to know each other

extremely well. To the point where at times I already know what Our Blessed Mother is going to say. I wish all of you could hear her most unique and loving soft voice I have been gifted to hear in the writing of this booklet.

4. But when the writing of this booklet comes to an end, I will still always be able to speak with her and that gives me some peace of mind.

5. I owe it to you to document my spiritual history and abilities so as to reassure you I am capable of performing the tasks Our Heavenly Father has asked me to perform in your behalf. Of this theological material out of my deep love for the Trinity and Blessed Mother Mary and especially for *__you__*, God's sacred children. Your Heavenly Father never makes mistakes, and he chose me to do this. I am completely honored and humbled he did choose me.

6. I will not fail Our Heavenly Father and I will not fail you his beloved sacred children.

7. One thing you should know, Satan has attacked me throughout my life. And while writing these theological materials your Heavenly Father wants me to, I'm forced to perform spiritual warfare every day, due to his attacks against me. Satan is a real pest.

There are other details about me and my life in both the spiritual and physical realms later on in this booklet. In conclusion, the bottom line is I am a sacred child of God just like you. But in my case Our Heavenly Father has chosen me to do some extraordinary things for the benefit of all others of his sacred children. And so, I will.

I love all of you sacred children ever so much,
Rich

Blessed Mother Mary Speaks

May 14, 2024
Blessed Mother Mary

Oh, my dearest of sons, how can I possibly thank you enough. For working so very hard. And revealing to your Heavenly Father's sacred children ever so much of the content of what I have been trying to communicate to His children for the last 500 years or more. It has been for me extremely difficult and frustrating. To bring forth the messages that our Father wants His sacred children to know about. As I have told you earlier, I have really had 375 apparitions each of which was intended to bring the love of your Almighty Father and the Trinity. But also tell this vitally essentially information, it is ever so sad for me to also have to bring the terrible warnings to God's children on earth.

As you know, my dear son, God's sacred children on earth are exposed purposely to Satan and all of his falsehoods and temptations. Each of you came to the earth to take what is known in the Heavenly Kingdom as the "earth test." This test has two features to it. The first is to experience your Heavenly Father in ways that go beyond what can be experienced in the Heavenly Kingdom. You will come to know your Heavenly Father in a far deeper and unique way than if you had chosen to stay in the spiritual realm in your home in the Heavenly Kingdom.

The second feature is you will be exposed to physical hardships and suffering on earth so as to evaluate your dedication and love for your Heavenly Father. Additionally, you will be exposed to so many different Satanic temptations that will include putting yourself above others of God's sacred children and even God Himself. Yes, you know dear son this will lead people to their ultimate destruction in hell.

My dear son you have become far stronger within the spiritual Kingdom because of all the suffering you have gone through. And now you are God's Anointed Messenger to bring His message of peace, love, understanding and acceptance of the Godly rules that exist on earth. Also, dearest son, you have done magnificently to explain to God's sacred children precisely how all of creation works and how it is tied together for the benefit of His sacred children.

Since I was born human on earth 2,000 years ago, I am able to bring much needed information to God's sacred children on earth. My messages of love can be found in my apparitions like the one at Lourdes. But even though it breaks my Heart, your Father asked me to bring messages of warning to His children on earth. This is because the large majority of His children have succumbed and given in to Satanic temptations. Most of them have abandoned Jesus Christ who is the way the truth and the life. No one goes to the Father except through Him. Over a period of time, the children on earth have rejected increasingly the one true God. And have fallen for physical sensual pleasures, adoration of Pagan Gods and given up true Godly morality replacing it with their imaginary rules that are invented so as to bring physical pleasure only. Once my dear son you have described the country you live in as a modern-day Sodom and Gomorrah.

You are so right, dear son. Ever so sadly dear son, you are also so very right when you said that your Democrat party is the political arm of Satan. If only people could stand back and look at what has been happening to your society through them and where the tragic events will continue to occur because of them. The destruction of your southern border is one example where tremendous pain and suffering is now just starting to happen to your society. Such that your country will become unrecognizable from every other sad country in the world just like what your former President Barack Obama has wanted. I remember dear son he said, "I see no reason why America should be any better than all the other countries in the world." Look to Canada and the tragedy unfolding there which is what will happen to your country if you do not turn to God.

It is for these reasons that I have come to earth and appeared to many people 375 times. So as to plant the seeds of Godly love to everyone who is willing to listen and live their lives accordingly. Because of my efforts and the unwillingness of people today to spread my words of love. And importantly of the warnings of what will come if they continue to turn their backs on the one true God, there will be many catastrophes from many different directions on earth.

Dear son, you have documented my warnings very well inside this booklet. And all the time and the efforts and the suffering you have gone through to bring this booklet to God's sacred children. The same milestone of love of you for your Heavenly Father and the Kingdom of Heaven.

The only the last thing I can say is I look forward so much to hug you and thank you upon your arrival within the Heavenly Kingdom.

I love you ever so much, Your Blessed Mother Mary

Thank you, dear Blessed Mother Mary! I love you too ever so very much! We will always continue our discussions.

My dear sacred child of God, this booklet you hold in your hands is a Sacred Document. It is so because it contains the direct words of our Blessed Mother Mary. All sacred words contained within will always be presented in bold and italicized print. My words as author and Anointed Messenger of our Heavenly Father will always be in regular Times New Roman text. Why is it this way? It is because Blessed Mother Mary is far more important than me God's Anointed Messenger.

This booklet contains a selected number of Mother Mary's apparitions that apply directly to the end of times that the earth has entered into. Signs of the End of Times are all over the earth if anyone cares to pay attention. This booklet will explore the prophecies made by our Blessed Mother Mary and how at this time they are increasingly being fulfilled.

It is her apparitions at Fatima, especially the third secret, that directly apply to the state of the world we are experiencing now. It is her apparitions from Fatima the Catholic Church tried to keep secret. This is because the truth of what Mother Mary had to say revealed awful Satanic things about the Catholic Church. Other apparitions we will discuss support Mother Mary's words in Fatima.

Now, in everything I say and write, the question will always remain why I should believe this author and what he says Mother Mary told him. The answer to that question is really quite simple. I ask you to pray directly to our Heavenly Father our lord and savior Jesus Christ and the holy spirit which proceeds from them. Ask them if what you are reading is true and correct. I am God's Messenger not God's sales associate. All I can do is to bring you the truth about the Trinity and Mother Mary says. I am not here to try and convince you of anything. Our Heavenly Father gave you free will and a magnificent capacity for logic, reason, and faith. If you use the tools that Our Heavenly Father gifted each of us with, you will come to understand everything within this Booklet and the others I have written are true.

I am our Father 's messenger and I will not engage in Christian apologetics. From the sacred words I bring, you will either come to a higher level of understanding and faith, or you will reject it. I always remember what Saint Thomas Aquinas said many years ago:

If You Have Faith and You Believe, No Proof Is Necessary
If You Don't Have Faith and Disbelieve, No Proof Is Possible

If you have questions or are confused about something within this booklet, I strongly encourage you to pray to Almighty God about that. It is in this way you can never ever go wrong. Remember as I described in the first booklet of this series titled, "God's Grand Design of All Creation for Your Redemption." Our Heavenly Father loves each of us. So very much that when we were created in the blink of an eye billions of years ago in the Heavenly Kingdom, he left part of Himself within our personal spiritual being. It is in this way Our Heavenly Father knows everything about us and will always hear every prayer we ever say. He has promised to each of us He will always answer every one of our prayers and questions.

2

Blessed Mother Mary's Revelations Never Heard Before

As <u>Spoken Directly to Me</u>, Our Father 's Anointed Messenger [1]

Yes, our Blessed Mother Mary does indeed speak directly to me regarding the topics in this sacred document. Over the many years since the life of our Lord and savior Jesus Christ, Blessed Mother Mary has spoken to many people. And has had many apparitions to a wide variety of people in the years since then. In fact, Mother Mary has appeared 375 times to various people across the world, far more than you have been led to believe. She has also had an ongoing relationship with Pope John Paul II as seen another example. Our Blessed Mother Mary will always choose to speak with selected dedicated Christians that love the Holy Trinity and of course Blessed Mother Mary herself.

Our Blessed Mother Mary has chosen to speak to me because your Heavenly Father has asked me to be His Anointed Messenger. My mission is to bring all of His sacred children His message of love, peace, acceptance. And advanced theology that brings far deeper understandings of not only the Trinity but also His creations and why they all exist. You can find that information in another book I have written last year in 2023 titled, <u>God's Grand Design of All Creation for Your Redemption.</u>

---

[1] Note: My dear sacred child of God, this book you hold in your hands is a <u>Sacred Document</u>. It is so because it contains the direct words of our Blessed Mother Mary. All sacred words contained within will always be presented in bold and italicized print. My words as author and <u>Anointed Messenger</u> of our Heavenly Father will always be in regular Times New Roman text.

My dear sacred children of God, <u>this book you are holding in your</u> <u>hands is no ordinary book. It is a sacred document.</u> Why? It is approved by God Our Heavenly Father and Blessed Mother Mary. It is sacred because it contains the direct words of our Almighty Heavenly Father and our Blessed Mother Mary. The contents of this book are in perfect alignment with our holy Bible. There are no incompatibilities. It centers around the magnificent apparitions of our Blessed Mother Mary and her messages to all of God's sacred children on earth. In very many ways Mother Mary is the link between the Heavenly realm and the physical realm on earth.

This book contains a selected number of Mother Mary's apparitions that apply very directly to the end of times that the earth has entered into. Signs of the End of Times are all over the earth if anyone cares to pay attention. This book will explore the prophecies made by our Blessed Mother Mary and how at this time they are increasingly being fulfilled. There have been all too many charlatans in the media claiming they know what is going to happen. A very few holy people do but the vast majority just want to sell you something. The very first part of this sacred document we'll focus on Mother Mary's apparitions at Fatima Portugal.

It is her apparitions at Fatima, especially the third secret, that directly apply to the state of the world we are experiencing now. It is her apparitions from Fatima the Catholic Church tried to keep secret. This is because the truth of what Mother Mary had to say revealed awful Satanic things about the Catholic Church. Other apparitions we will discuss support Mother Mary's words in Fatima.

On page 2, you have read the exact words of our Heavenly Almighty Father spoken to me as a message to all of His sacred children. This means you. Not only does this book bring the message from Almighty God, a message of love, of understanding, acceptance, and advanced theological understandings as revealed by our Blessed Mother Mary.

The contents of this sacred book will indeed shock many of you. Much of the content of the secrets of Fatima is very upsetting yet we have been living in the beginning of the end of times since 1960.

Lately Pope Francis claimed he "finally revealed the entire contents of the third secret of Fatima" <u>Pope Francis is a damned Satanic liar</u>. Included later within this book are the Pope's so called total revelation word for word. After that are the exact words of our Blessed Mother Mary who revealed the third secret to the three shepherd kids at Fatima. Sister Lucia is the child that wrote down Mother Mary's words. They DO NOT match with Pope Francis at all. More on that later.

Most Christians think of our Blessed Mother Mary as the Mother of God and who appears on occasion in apparitions with children emphasizing the need for prayer, sacrifice, penance and praying the rosary.

I am fortunate enough to be one of the people Our Blessed Mother Mary wishes to talk to. In my case it is for writing the books that contain the messages of our holy Father in Heaven, our Lord and Savior Jesus Christ and of course Our Blessed Mother Mary.

As our Father's Anointed Messenger, it is my holy mission to bring God's truth of all creation to you His sacred children. I will do this until as Jesus Christ told me, until I rejoin Him in the Heavenly Kingdom. The following text explains in some detail how I became our Heavenly Father s Anointed Messenger. The process of becoming the Anointed Messenger started before I was born to this earth.

Now, in everything I say and write, the question will always remain why I should believe this author and what he says Mother Mary told him. The answer to that question is really quite simple. I ask you to pray directly to our Heavenly Father our lord and savior Jesus Christ and the Holy Spirit which proceeds from them. Ask them if what you are reading is true and correct. I am God's Messenger not God's sales associate. All I can do is to tell you the truth about the Trinity and Mother Mary says. I am not here to try and convince you of anything. Our Heavenly Father gave you free will and a magnificent capacity for logic, reason, and faith. If you use the tools Our Heavenly Father gifted each of us with, you will come to understand that everything within this book and the others I have written are true.

I am Our Father's Messenger and I will not engage in Christian apologetics. From the sacred words I bring, you will either come to a higher level of understanding and faith, or you will reject it. I always remember what Saint Thomas Aquinas said many years ago:

If You Have Faith and You Believe, No Proof Is Necessary
If You Don't Have Faith and Disbelieve, No Proof Is Possible

If you have questions or are confused about something within this book, I strongly encourage you to pray to Almighty God about that. It is in this way you can never ever go wrong. Remember as I described in the first book of this series titled, "God's Grand Design of All Creation for Your Redemption." Our Heavenly Father loves each of us. So very much that when we were created in the blink of an eye billions of years ago in the Heavenly Kingdom, he left part of Himself within our personal spiritual being. It is in this way Our Heavenly Father knows everything about us and will always hear every prayer we ever say. He has promised each of us he will always answer every one of our prayers and questions.

Becoming God's Anointed Messenger

I was born to earth as an only child. I was not wanted by either of my parents. To them I was just and irritating obstacle. My father was a cruel violent man, and my mother never lifted a finger to stop him from beating me for the slightest transgression as a small little boy. Years after leaving home and becoming Our Father's Anointed Messenger, Jesus told me my father was there to do everything he could to stop me from fulfilling my life's mission. A mission as was agreed to between me and our Almighty Father in Heaven. Yes, our Lord and Savior speaks to me. Satan wanted to destroy me through the cruelty of my own father. Satan failed. One of the characteristics of the spiritual realm is there are NO secrets, which means Satan knew and knows my purpose in this life. He wanted my father to destroy me and my mission on earth. He failed and he is now in hell.

Sometime after he died, he tried to come up from under the floor to me four times. And each time, I told him to go back to hell where he belongs in the name of our Lord and Savior Jesus Christ. Speaking of this, all Christians should know <u>they have authority over Satan</u>. Just tell them to go back to hell in the name of our Lord and savior Jesus Christ. And then say one our Father and Hail Mary and thank our Father in Heaven for your power over Satan.

During my late 40's I started to feel an ever-increasing yearning in my life to know God far better than I did. Every day I felt this increasing emptiness within me I knew only our Heavenly Father could fulfill. By then in my life, a number of spiritual events have already occurred. This supported my growing need through fundamentally "come to God."

At the time I worked in corporate computer marketing for Hewlett Packard corporation. I had a travel schedule worldwide. This conflicted with my class schedule in the master's degree in Pastoral Ministry and Theology. But the university was very accommodating, and this gave me the opportunity to work extremely hard to receive my degree.

I later found out from Jesus I had a conversation with our Loving Father in the Heavenly Kingdom about my coming life on earth. That discussion determined my life theme when I was born to the earth. My life theme is amazingly simple. I wanted to put every other one of God's sacred children ahead of me and I would serve them. I would serve others of God's sacred children by bringing advanced understandings of our Father's creations to them. However, Jesus Christ pointed out to me this is one of the most difficult life themes for sacred children coming to earth. Satan hated this. One point of education for you about the spiritual realm is there are no secrets, whatsoever. Everybody knows everything about everybody else. Please ponder on this.

Satan Attacks Me Viciously Three Times

This is something Satan hated terribly about me, and he would want to destroy anybody that has such a loving God centered theme in their earthly life. <u>The one most terrible experience I had was when Satan attacked me three times in the middle of the night</u>. This occurred on three separate occasions. There was a loud crash within the house as if it is a car crashed through my home and into the living room.

When Satan himself invaded my bedroom where my wife and I were sleeping, and my two small children were sleeping in the next bedroom I thought all hell broke loose. There was the most horrific crashing banging sound I could ever imagine in the middle of the night. When I looked up toward the foot of the bed there stood Satan himself. There can be no doubt. Remember Satan can be only one place at a time. And there he was standing at the foot of our bed staring at me with his glowing red eyes. With that and his body bent over such I had to look up almost vertical to see his head and red eyes hovering over me. Then he yelled at me these words, "at the top of his ugly voice he yelled at me three times. He said" **I will get you! I will get you! I will get you!"** After yelling this at me with his booming loud voice when his head was no more than two feet from my nose, he leaned backward to straighten himself. He continued to stare at me for some more long seconds. Then with the audible whoosh he departed my bedroom to the left. He went straight through the wall as if it did not exist. Silence and peace returned to our bedroom.

I will leave it there for this is a booklet about Blessed Mother Mary, not me.

The Beginning of My Christian Spiritual Warfare

Since then, Satan has harassed me every day of my life. When I am engaging in the sacred writing of the books, Our Heavenly Father wants me to write for His sacred children to read. Satan would be there throwing rotten thoughts into my brain so as to distract me and conduct harassment. I was forced to conduct spiritual warfare. As a wicked example, I'd be in the middle of writing a sentence in a book to be published and out of nowhere I would hear a terrible thought enter my conscience like F*ck God! Very unsettling. I then have to command Satan to leave me in the name of our Lord and Savior Jesus

Christ, say an Our Father and Hail Mary. That gets rid of Satan but is yet another harassment from him.

I must tell you this dear sacred child of God, to battle Satan is not as hard as you think. Is it scary? Yes at least at the beginning. But after a while it gets to be routine. If you are on good terms with our loving Father, our Lord and savior Jesus Christ and the Holy Spirit which proceeds from them it is relatively easy. Every time when I am writing and Satan tries to interfere, I just simply stop what I am doing calmly then I say one Our Father and one Hail Mary. Then I command Satan to leave me, to depart me and go back to hell where he belongs in the name of our Lord and savior Jesus Christ and our Blessed Mother Mary.

The Unexpected Arrival of Jesus Christ and Blessed Mother Mary

I seriously do NOT want this booklet to be about me. But given the role I have at the request of our Heavenly Father; I feel you need to understand just whose words you are reading.

When I was approximately 70 years old, I was meditating after I got up and swung my feet over the side of the bed. I notice something very strange occurring about forty feet away in front of me. There were two spiritual entities there just standing there and looking at me. It was easy to see one was a male with brown hair and white robes. The other person was definitely female with blue and white robes and a blue hood over the top of her head. She was shorter than the male. The first time I saw this having been experienced at seeing other spiritual beings, it was not that big a deal to me, but it got my attention. After a few seconds I went about my business for the day. The next day I woke up and I noticed these same two spiritual persons looking the same but being a little closer to me than the previous day before.

Well that certainly got my attention. Something was up but I had no idea what it was. But I had things to do, and I resumed my daily activities. On the third day when I woke up and swung my feet over the right side of the bed, these two spiritual people were still closer than the previous night and the one before that. They still remained silent but now I knew something was really up, but I still did not know what. On the fourth day they were no more than five or six feet from me in front and to my right side. Strangely I was almost certain I knew who they were at this point, but I did not dare say anything, at least not yet. I was beginning to think these two spiritual people were Jesus Christ and our Blessed Mother Mary. Naw, that cannot be or so I thought.

Now the fifth morning arises. My darling wife Evangeline already was up and somewhere in the house. It was a morning like no other in my entire life. When I woke up laying down and staring at the ceiling, I did not see them. I wondered where they went. Soon I was to find out in a matter of seconds. In the act of swinging my legs over the side of the bed, the gaze of my eyes caught the unmistakable image of our Lord and Savior Jesus Christ and our Beloved Blessed Mother Mary. They were silently standing right next to my right shoulder. Perhaps 4 to 6 inches away from me. This shocked the heck out of me. I did not know what to do, I did not know what to say, I did not know anything to do in any way. I was completely stunned. There I was, my feet hanging over the side of the bed with two Biblical sentient spiritual beings standing right next to me on my right side.

I started to go into a state of shock. But I had enough presence of mind to ask the following question in a telepathic way I have used many times before speaking with spiritual beings: I asked, "**Are you who I think you are?**" Jesus answered with these exact words, "***Yes, It Is I.***" Instantly I thought it strange he did not say "it is me." Because that is the incorrect English everybody uses. Proper English is exactly what Jesus said." ***Yes, It is I.***"

With that response from Jesus, everything and I mean absolutely everything within all of my senses turned completely white. All my surroundings in the bedroom completely disappeared. They were gone. I no longer felt I was sitting on the edge of my bed. There was no sensation at all. The ceiling was gone the floors were gone; the bed I was sitting on was gone. There was no sound replaced by complete silence. The only things that existed was my consciousness, my identity, and an awareness of who I was with and where I thought I was but apparently not anymore. Instantly, the only awareness I had was I existed, and our Lord and savior Jesus Christ and Mother Mary were close by my right side. There was nothing else. There was absolutely no fear.

The next thing I heard was dear Lord Jesus telling me to put my feet back up on the bed and just rest and remain calm as much as I can. I did but, in the process, I didn't see my legs anymore. I don't remember feeling them either, nor did I see the rest of the bed or the rest of the bedroom for that matter.

It was just me, our loving Lord Jesus Christ, and our Beloved Mother Mary. Nothing else!

After an unknown time resting on the bed. Jesus told me to just keep laying down and listen to what he wanted to tell me. He said Mother Mary and He are there to help me with the coming things our Heavenly Father wants me to do for the rest of His sacred children on earth. I do not remember His exact words but that is the central idea.

Jesus also told me both He and Mother Mary would stay with me by my side forever more. They will never leave me. I felt wonderful hearing that.

After this encounter, our Lord, and Savior Jesus Christ and. Our Blessed Mother Mary were indeed at my right-hand side 100% of every waking moment of my life. I can see them in full living color. They are with me always, and they know absolutely everything about my existence, including what I was thinking, what I was feeling, what was happening to me and everything else directly associated with my existence. Today they remain indeed always with me by my side. There was never a moment I could not see them, but rather I can always see Jesus with our Blessed Mother Mary in her blue and white robes, and our Lord and savior Jesus Christ. To this day as I write this sentence, I can clearly see both of them standing no more than six inches from my right shoulder.

Frankly at first this whole thing was quite unnerving. But after a while I started asking Jesus a lot of questions about so many different theological topics. He is always ever so happy to answer anything I wanted to know. It is through this personal tutoring of our Lord

Jesus I learned ever so much about creation and about all the details related to how creation works together through its individual facets of existence.

It is through the private tutoring of Our Lord and Savior Jesus Christ along with our Blessed Mother Mary that gave me the most magnificent information about all of creation. Both in the spiritual realm and the physical realm allowing me to write the master Booklet ***"God's Grand Design of All Creation for Your Redemption."*** I didn't rely on other resources like online or YouTube because why would I do that when Jesus Christ is the one that did indeed create the entire physical realm, we call the universe.

And the preceding full-sized book, <u>God's Grand Design, Blessed Mother Mary Speaks, Her Apparitions and The End of Time</u>. I give a detailed description of how it came to be where our Lord and savior of Jesus Christ and our blessed mother Mary approached me and are now with me 100% of the time. They are always standing beside me by my right shoulder, and each has their left hand on my left shoulder and the other on my right shoulder.

Question: Dearest Mother Mary, during the time you and Jesus were approaching me for the first time would you comment please on what it is you were thinking about all of that? Jesus did do all the talking and I would really like to know what your thoughts were as a you and my savior approached me for the first time.

Answer: *Of course, my dearest son, I felt this certain amount of trepidation because we did not know exactly how you would react. We know your love for your Heavenly Father and Jesus, the Holy Spirit and me was very great. But we needed to be very gentle with you because the last thing we wanted was to in some way as you would say "scared the pants off you." You have had many spiritual experiences in your life already before we approached you. And that was an exceptionally good thing. Because of your experiences that ranged from the elders on the cruise ship praying for your late wife Marilyn to Satan Himself trying to scare the living daylights out of you. There were so many other incidents that we felt this would be* *one more spiritual experience for you that would not damage you in any way. This is what we were very afraid of with any sacred child of God still living in their physical body.*

It was your love for God and for me that made me feel you are the only right person. With all your experiences academically with your degrees in chemistry and physics. And being a pilot, which demands certain amount of perfection and discipline. And the way that you brought up your children within the Catholic faith. And their education. And that you are the leader of your family bringing them up in the right way. Along with then you getting your master's degree in ministry and theology we knew that you had all the necessary qualifications to do what it is your Heavenly Father has asked you to.

I felt strongly that you would say yes to your Heavenly Father. So too did Jesus my son. I will never forget before Satan attacked you those three times when you were yelling at him for making a mess on earth that you repeated those terrible swearwords aimed at him. It showed us that you were just not afraid, and you were a fighter. When Our Heavenly Father joined you on the airplane. When you were halfway across the Pacific Ocean and He told you that he was happy you were a fighter right after Satan attacked you in your airline seat. You just reconfirmed everything we thought that you would become. And you have become everything we wished plus a lot more.

It is particularly good that you asked me this question. Because all these sacred children of your Heavenly Father when they read this will understand just how close all of us are together. Which includes everyone of God's sacred children also as you have demonstrated throughout this Booklet many times. I love the fact that you speak your mind in truly clear forceful terms. And in addition to you being a fighter you also have all the protections of the Heavenly realm right by your side.

My dearest of sons. I love you so very very much. And, in a way, I hope that we can just keep writing and writing this booklet, but I know it must come to an end sometime soon. But I will always be with you right by your side along with my son for that is timeless and will never end.

   I love you dear son.
   Mother Mary

Why Me Lord?

During the time I was writing that book, this question came to me. After a while I began to wonder, "why me?" Why is it Our Heavenly Father chose me? Out of all the others of God's sacred children within the universe He asked of all people to be the Anointed Messenger and write this ever so important book? The most important book that will become recognized as a sacred book in the eyes of the Christian community along with the Old Testament and the New Testament.

I asked Jesus that exact question. **WHY ME?** Jesus once told me sometime last year Our Heavenly Father chose me to be His Anointed Messenger because of <u>something I said to Him</u>. First dear sacred children of God, all of you were in the Heavenly Kingdom BEFORE you came to earth. All of us could talk with our Heavenly Father. Well, that really got my attention. What on earth could I possibly have said? And the other thought I had was, "oh good grief, me and my big mouth!" Sometimes I tend to do that.

Yep. That was my instantaneous thought when Jesus told me that. After I gathered myself a little bit, I asked our Lord what did I say? Jesus told me that before my upcoming earthly life I told Our Heavenly Father I wanted to put other people ahead of myself while I was in my upcoming life on earth. This would be my lifetime theme as all of us do have a life theme. Jesus then told me that this is a particularly difficult life to live. Boy, was he right! Maybe I will write an article about that. At this point though I think I should terminate anymore thoughts about how I became our Heavenly Father's Anointed Messenger. I have already spent too much time away from our Blessed Mother Mary.

There is one thought I wish to leave you with. Regarding my lifetime on earth as a chosen one, I know Our Heavenly Father is within me just as he is within every sacred child of His on earth. This means YOU! Yes, you, as everybody are a sacred child of Almighty God. All sacred children are made in the image of God. This is why Satan hates every one of us. If you were a rabbit, he would not care. In another book I will write, I'll describe in detail the trials and tribulations in my life caused by hateful Satan against me because he knew our Father chose me as His Anointed Messenger.

Regarding our Blessed Mother Mary, it was she and our Lord and Savior Jesus Christ that approached me some years ago now. They told me they would be with me forever by my side. My dearest sacred children of God, I cannot begin to tell you how beautiful and magnificent it is to see Lord and Savior Jesus Christ and Blessed Mother Mary right beside me. Always slightly behind my right shoulder. And yes, dear sacred children I can see them in living color.

This is why parts of this book centering upon Our Blessed Mother Mary, you'll read her pointing to her instantaneous knowledge of how I am physically feeling. How tired I can get and many times becoming exhausted. Even though our Mother Mary is now a pure spiritual being, she retains the ability to know and understand my feelings within my physical body.

3

All About Our
Blessed Mother Mary

I know very well that most of you will have doubts or reject what I have just written. This rejection has been proven over many years considering how the message from our Lord and Savior Jesus Christ was received 2,000 years ago. Surprisingly to me the same thing happened to our Blessed Mother Mary over hundreds of years with her loving apparitions. She told me she appeared 375 times, but we know of only a few. She "laments" about this. People were either scared, disbelieving, or unwilling to tell other people what Mother Mary told them. Let us take her apparition at Fatima. That became a Vatican political football where the Church officials became horrifically political and now Pope Francis just last month as this is written TOLD FALSEHOODS about the third secret. He bold face TOLD a FALSEHOOD that the third sacred has been fulfilled and Russia has been consecrated to the Immaculate Heart of Blessed Mother Mary. NO! NO! and NO! again! Francis is a liar! He made it look like that, but he did not say the proper words as shown in another part of this booklet.

Another roadblock was the Catholic Church itself. The general attitude of the Church was deep skepticism, disbelief, and outright hiding things from our Father's sacred children. This last action by the Church is what they did to the third secret of Fatima as told by our Blessed Mother Mary. They did so because the third secret was extremely powerful and made the Catholic Church look really bad. As you will see herein, you will read all the contents of the third secret and judge the Church for yourselves.

Without going into detail, suffice to say Our Heavenly Father through Jesus Christ and Blessed Mother Mary asked me to write a booklet. One that delivers our Father's message of love, peace, understanding and acceptance to His sacred children on earth. Additionally, Father provided advanced theological information that addresses advanced existential understandings of how all His creation is designed, how it works and where we as Father's sacred children fit into things. Everything in these advanced theological understandings is completely consistent with our Blessed Holy Bible. The title is: <u>God's Grand Design of All Creation for Your Redemption.</u> It begins by answers to the question of what exactly are you. The answer is magnificently beautiful.

Remember, each and every one of you is a sacred child of Almighty God. You are a spiritual being living on earth for specific reasons I will not go into now. I have written a booklet titled, "<u>God's Grand Design Booklet I Creation</u>." It is here I have written everything your Heavenly Father wants you to know about your existence. Everything written there is completely consistent with our Christian Biblical literature.

We will start with La Salette, then continue with Garabandal, Lourdes, Zeitoun and finally to Fatima. But first I feel it is very revealing and appropriate I describe what our Blessed Mother Mary's voice sounds like. In a nutshell it is beautiful.

How Does Blessed Mother Mary Speak with Me?

The manner in which Mother Mary's thoughts wind up in a sacred booklet like this is actually pretty simple. Given Our Heavenly Father appointed me as His anointed messenger, which brings with it the ability to speak with the Holy Trinity and our Blessed Mother Mary. Yes, that last sentence is absolutely true but also exceedingly rare.

At the direct request of our holy Almighty Father, I wrote a Booklet that contains what our Father wants all of His sacred children to know. The title is, "<u>God's Grand Design of All Creation for Your Redemption</u>." Now Blessed Mother Mary is articulating deep details of the End of Times and five of Her apparitions where she describes the horrific times mankind has entered into starting back in

1960. I am helping Her write this booklet with all the information she wants to tell all of our Heavenly Father's sacred children.

The Sacred Process

When it is appropriate I will cloister myself in an incredibly quiet room within my home. I must create the physical conditions necessary so my prayer for all attention centers on our beloved and Blessed Mother Mary. I pray the Our Father and Hail Mary. Additionally, I will pray as much of the rosary as is necessary to completely eliminate any distracting earthly thoughts that may have been bothering me. There are times when I have to conduct spiritual warfare against Satan. He hates me more than you can imagine.

Nonetheless, I am protected. And when I'm peaceful within and my attention drifts to Our Blessed Mother Mary, I'm ready to ask her questions and invite her to tell me anything she wants God's sacred children to know.

This is such a beautiful and sacred thing to do, preparing to speak with actually not only our Blessed Mother Mary but also our Lord and savior Jesus Christ. Additionally on more rare occasions I will want to ask our loving Heavenly Father a question or two. But what usually happens is I will be engaging in some activity and our Heavenly Father starts talking to me at His will not mine. I remember one time I was away from my computer and our Heavenly Father started to speak with me. I was forced to respond by saying, Dear Father, please wait for a moment until I can get my speech to text software up and running. So, I can make sure everything you say will be preserved for all your sacred children.

While I was preparing the computer and turning on the software, I thought to myself, "good Lord Richard, do you realize what you just did? You actually ask our loving creator of all that is seen and unseen to wait a minute for you? How awful can you get? But our loving Father waited for the minute or two and then I said, "dear Father I'm ready please tell me anything you wish." And within a fleeting moment that is exactly what He did. I will never forget that moment as long as I live and actually for all eternity when I am back into the Kingdom.

The Reason Mother Mary Speaks to Me

The reason is so important I tell you how my position with the Trinity and Blessed Mother Mary came about. Because everything has been published with regards to our Blessed Mother Mary's apparitions is always second-hand and third-hand. All of it loaded with opinions that many times are completely misguided and based upon only partial information. This does a terrible service to God's sacred children which is YOU!

Additionally, (I'll complain about this later) the Catholic Church has proven a roadblock to God's sacred children from hearing firsthand and accurate content of the messages Our Blessed Mother Mary has bestowed upon us. This is especially true with Fatima.

What you hold in your hand has NO INTERFERENCES from the Catholic Church or any other people who wish to manipulate the words of our Blessed Mother Mary. One case in point. Mother Mary asked that the third secret of Fatima be delivered to all of God's sacred children in the year of 1960. That never happened. Why? It is because the third secret does indeed reveal terrible things that will happen to the earth unless mankind repents. But importantly the third secret reveals the vast corruption, apostasy, blasphemy, sexual perversion, and even Satanic worship within the Vatican. Yes, you read that correctly!

I have included other apparitions within this sacred document because of two reasons:

1. Mother Mary asked me to
2. The content of these apparitions all fit together to produce a picture of the future of God's sacred children on earth. That future is referred to as "The End of Times."

This will all be discussed openly and plainly within this booklet. Jesus Christ Himself said, "I am the way the truth and the life and no one goes to the Father except by me." Well, the Church has been fighting the release of the truth Blessed Mother Mary has been trying to deliver to God's sacred children for many hundreds of years. The Church has gone so far astray for example as to create a fake Lucia of Fatima so as to drastically water down the true message of Fatima. At least this is what significant evidence shows along with experts that have scientifically proven the lady posing as Lucia today is not the real historical Lucia.

This Booklet contains the authentic words of our Blessed Mother Mary as she wants everyone of God's sacred children to hear firsthand. Many priests, nuns, bishops, and Cardinals have all been sworn to secrecy. So, they have been muffled by the Vatican and other Church powers to prevent you from hearing about what you should know. I HAVE NOT TAKEN ANY OATH OF ANY KIND! So, this booklet will deliver all of Blessed Mother Mary's messages through her apparitions to God's sacred children, YOU! Fundamentally this means the words of our Blessed Mother Mary are going directly from her to you through the printed words in this booklet.

She will do this directly. How? It is because your Heavenly Father has asked me to be His Anointed Messenger. As His Anointed Messenger I have been gifted to be able to talk with Blessed Mother Mary directly. Yes! I have been magnificently gifted by our loving Father in Heaven to be able to talk directly with our Blessed Mother Mary and our Lord and savior Jesus Christ. Additionally, our Heavenly Father speaks to me very clearly about assorted items that come up regarding the publication of the booklets he wants to be written and published for your benefit.

Previous to this booklet, I have written a small booklet titled, "God's Grand Design, Booklet I Creation." I suggest you get a copy. Our Father wants you to know what is contained there. Regarding this Booklet, there is no intermediary. Whatever Blessed Mother Mary tells me directly, I transcribe it directly to my computer where a text file is generated. This text file contains the exact words of whatever Blessed Mother Mary tells me.

There are no filters, no priests or bishops or Cardinals or other Church related people that will get in the way and pervert and twist the truth of what Blessed Mother Mary has said. She wants everybody to know about the coming times and especially the End of Times which are upon us right now. Since approximately 1960 the world has entered the End of Times. More on that later in this booklet.

So, what you're about to read is the unfiltered, untwisted, unedited and unmodified words of our Blessed Mother Mary in the messages she has been trying to get out to all of God's sacred children. Therefore, you must realize that this booklet is sacred from the first page to the last period on the last page. It is sacred truth as said directly by our Blessed Mother Mary, the Mother of God, the Mother of our Lord and savior Jesus Christ.

The Beautiful Voice of Mother Mary

I have never seen a description of what Blessed Mother Mary's voice sounds like throughout all my research from many diverse sources that claim to have heard what she says in her apparitions. I don't know why this is because her voice is remarkably distinctive and divine. I have had the beautiful experience of hearing her melodies of language many times during the course of writing this booklet. Imagine a loving human based Heavenly Angelic female voice in your mind, you would be describing Blessed Mother Mary in her fullness of love and gentleness for each and every one of God's sacred children.

I can describe her voice as ever so feminine and gentle speaking slowly and softly with caressing a sincere love that projects a magnificent divine quality to what she says. Her voice with its softness and its ever so caring tone of love really does gently soothe my mind and it makes me feel so wonderfully loved.

Her divine love for me feels like it is contained in every word she says. When she speaks of warnings to all of God's sacred children like the third secret of Fatima, there is a tone of urgency and deep concern in her voice. One beautiful characteristic of how Blessed Mother speaks is that when she wants to emphasize a word, she stretches out the word more than the others. For example, if she wants to say, "that is a real problem," it will sound like she is stretching out that phrase a little longer than normal. Poetically speaking her voice is like a soft breeze rustling through the trees with a love that defies description. Her loving and lilting voice is like a divine touch to my soul. Oh, how I wish each of you could hear with your own ears our Blessed Mother Mary. But, one day you will after you enter the paradise we call the Heavenly Kingdom.

She is never at a loss for words and when she explains something she also includes related thoughts that amplify what she means. She knows me ever so well. There have been times, actually many times, when I suffer from my chronic migraine headaches and am in a lot of pain when I want to speak with her. She knows how I feel and many times she suggests we delay our conversation and I need to have rest for a time. I take my strong pain medicine and after a while I feel better, and Mother Mary knows that and then we continue what we intended to begin with.

There have been times also when I have been very tired many times from headache pain and even though the pain is gone, I'm just exhausted and even Mother Mary knows this too. And even then, she suggests I rest. She has told me to rest so many times because Our Lord and Savior Jesus Christ told her I work too hard especially when I was sick for two months early in the year 2024.

April 17, 2024
Our Beloved Blessed Mother Mary:

My dearest son Richard, you have worked so extremely hard to bring the truth of our Holy Father to His sacred children on earth. You are so very correct that our Father's sacred children have now entered into <u>The End of Times</u>. As you have observed, dearest son. That falling away from the love and the rules of life that Our Father has put forth for the benefit and the happiness of His children on earth has been under increasing attack by Satan. As you have said, you have observed the crumbling away of God's manner of living on earth so as to return to Him in the Heavenly Kingdom for all eternity.

Especially dear son, your Booklet titled <u>God's Grand Design of All Creation For Your Redemption</u>, is a magnificent piece of Biblical literature that you have written in common everyday *language so everybody can understand. It is slowly gaining in popularity and will continue as such. I am honored dear son, dear Anointed Messenger of our Father, to be with you writing about my apparitions throughout the many years until now.*

One thing I want your readers to know is that in your research you have found that there have been about thirty-four apparitions of me mostly to little children. I have chosen little children because they have not been in the world long enough to become jaded, and their minds are still fresh, close to their Heavenly Father and honest. But in some cases, as you have found out like La Salette in France, the children became afraid due to the elders that surrounded them. Maximin could not stand the pressure and revoked saying that he told a falsehood. He did not. Both you and I know this.

Other things that people do not realize is that I have appeared to many others since my son was on the earth. In actual fact my dear son, I have appeared many times more than the 34 apparitions that have been published to be read by God's sacred children in the Church. Most of the time the children that I appeared to after a time became exceedingly frightened and did not tell anyone of what occurred. My message to everyone is always ever so simple. It is basically love, peace, penance, sacrifice and to always say the Holy Rosary.

People continue to not understand the Almighty power of what I have just mentioned. Why is this so? It is because doing these things strengthens enormously people's love and connection directly to the Trinity and me. This strong connection destroys Satan's ability to cause agony, pain, suffering in the world. Basically, the closer you are to your Heavenly Father, the farther away Satan becomes. Satan's violence and destructive temptations do not stand a chance against prayer, sacrifice, penance, and the Holy Rosary.

This is why in doing these things great spiritual power comes to all those who listen to what I have to say. With this spiritual power across many people in the world, ever so many wars in the world would be avoided.

However, the time of Satan is at hand. To you my dearest Anointed Messenger of our Holy Father, what you have said that the world has now entered into the preliminary stages of the end of times. You have also stated that you know Satan is working within the Vatican and yes, my dear son Pope France is under the control of Satan and is the last pope. Frightening as this may be, things will get worse before they get better. In another part of this Booklet you are writing, I will expand upon my prophecies all of which will come true before my son will return to earth.

A horrific number of lives and souls will be lost in the coming years. Dear son I suggest you at this time document all the wars in the world right now. It is Heartbreaking yet I knew all of this would happen and so now you too.

Let us, you, and I, now proceed with far more details in this magnificent Booklet and I want you to center upon my apparitions that talk about the End of Times.

I love you ever so much my dearest son. You are protected and always in my prayers.

Your Blessed Mother Mary

Question: If you don't mind, me being so quantitative. Could you put a numerical figure on just how many times you appeared to different children in separate places on earth to deliver your messages and your warnings?

Answer: *Oh, of course dear son I will. You may be surprised but remember I also have appeared without saying anything to anybody. It is my image of love and peace that appears to people to remind them of not only me but my messages of love, peace, sacrifice, prayer, the mass, and the powerful Rosary. These are too numerous to mention because ever so many thousands of people see my image but then my effect on their prayer life slowly fades away.*

But regarding the times in which I have spoken to selected ones of God's sacred children and have not been reported. The number you are looking for is 375 times that I have spoken to the sacred children of God. My appearance almost always produces fear among the children. Many times, they do not report what they saw because of their fear of getting into trouble with the elders. Other times elders ignore what they say thinking they are just making up fanciful stories. Even when the children describe my appearances to the parents and local elders all along with in the contents of what I have said. The event gets tangled up and confused by people in the Church.

Many times, even the local priests and bishops accused the children of lying and this is what happened at La Salette. They reported what they saw and what was said. One of the children disappeared from the scene and the other, Maximin simply denied our encounter and said he told a falsehood. However, there are particularly important and shining examples of when things mostly go right and the legitimate appearance of mine reaches the higher authorities in the Church. But even then, due to the honest content like in Fatima, the Church hierarchy decides to hide my words of prophecy because they think it makes the Church look bad. Lastly, Garabandal, Akita and Medjugorje are good examples of things going properly and I would like you to emphasize these in this magnificent Booklet you are writing.

People, God's sacred children must know what is coming and that things have already started that are part of the End of Times. This is not the end of the world; it is the End of Times which will be horrifically painful in so many ways that I will tell you later in this terrific Booklet.

Mother Mary, The Link Between Earth and Heaven

Most people believe Mother Mary is the Mother of Jesus Christ and was raised up to Heaven by God. Some people know she has had apparitions that are miraculous. Beyond that, people do not know much. The fact is Mother Mary is extremely active in her sacred attempts to bring redemption to all of God sacred children. You will be amazed at everything she has done and is currently doing to bring about a Heavenly future for as many of God's sacred children on earth as she possibly can.

I bring you the below information because its message is twofold and enormously powerful. Most Christians think of our Blessed Mother Mary as the Mother of God and who appears on occasion in apparitions with children emphasizing the need for prayer, sacrifice, penance and praying the rosary. Our Mother Mary plays an active role in helping those of goodwill to avoid catastrophes on earth.

Her importance goes far deeper than just that, if that isn't enough. Our Blessed Mother Mary also maintains holy friendships and communications with people who are still on earth. The below story about Pope John II talking with her and abiding by what she asks him to do. This is so powerful and goes way beyond apparitions. Remember please, it is our Blessed Mother Mary that will put an end to Satan by virtue of her magnificent love and her Immaculate Heart! It is our Blessed Mother Mary's Immaculate Heart that will crush the head of Satan. How? It is by her Immaculate intense love.

I am fortunate enough to be one of the people Our Blessed Mother Mary wishes to talk to. In my case it is for writing the books that contain the messages of our holy Father in Heaven, our Lord and Savior Jesus Christ and of course our Blessed Mother Mary. This book is completely dedicated to our Blessed Mother Mary.

March 14, 2024
Spoken by our Almighty Father's Anointed Messenger

My dear sacred child of God, this book you hold in your hands is a Sacred Document. It is so because it contains the direct words of our Blessed Mother Mary. All sacred words contained within will always be presented in bold and italicized print. My words as author and Anointed Messenger of our Heavenly Father will always be in regular Times New Roman text. Why is it this way? It is because Blessed Mother Mary is far more important than me God's Anointed Messenger.

Here is the first of many things Mother Mary will say within this Book.

April 17, 2024

Our Beloved Blessed Mother Mary:

My dearest son Richard, you have worked so extremely hard to bring the truth of our Holy Father to His sacred children on earth. You are so very correct that our Father's sacred children have now entered into <u>The End of Times</u>. As you have observed, dearest son, that falling away from the love and the rules of life that our Father has put forth for the benefit and the happiness of His children on earth. Has been under increasing attack by Satan. As you have said, you have observed the crumbling away of God's manner of living on earth so as to return to Him in the Heavenly Kingdom for all eternity.

Especially dear son, your book titled <u>God's Grand Design of All Creation for Your Redemption</u>, is a magnificent piece of Biblical literature that you have written in common everyday language so everybody can understand. It is slowly gaining in popularity and will continue as such. I am honored dear son, dear Anointed Messenger of our Father, to be with you writing about my apparitions throughout the many years until now.

One thing I want your readers to know is that in your research you have found that there have been about thirty-four apparitions of me, mostly to little children. I have chosen little children because they have not been in the world long enough to become jaded, and their minds are still fresh, close to their Heavenly Father and honest. But in some cases, as you have found out like La Salette in France, the children became afraid due to the elders that surrounded them. Maximin could not stand the pressure and revoked saying that he told a falsehood. He did not. Both you and I know this.

Another thing that people do not realize is that I have appeared to many others since my son was on the earth. In actual fact, my dear son, I have appeared many times more than the 34 apparitions that have been published to be read by God's sacred children in the Church. Most of the time the children that I appeared to after a time became exceedingly frightened and did not tell anyone of what occurred. My message to everyone is always ever so simple. It is basically love, peace, penance, sacrifice and to always say the Holy Rosary.

People continue to not understand the Almighty power of what I have just mentioned. Why is this so? It is because doing these things strengthens enormously people's love and connection directly to the Trinity and me. This strong connection destroys Satan's ability to cause agony, pain, suffering in the world. Basically, the closer you are to your Heavenly Father, the farther away Satan becomes. Satan's violence and destructive temptations do not stand a chance against prayer, sacrifice, penance, and the Holy Rosary.

This is why in doing these things great spiritual power comes to all those who listen to what I have to say. With this spiritual power across many people in the world, ever so many wars in the world would be avoided.

However, the time of Satan is at hand. To you my dearest Anointed Messenger of our Holy Father, what you have said is that the world has now entered into the preliminary stages of the end of times. You have also stated that you know Satan is working within the Vatican and yes, my dear son Pope France is under the control of Satan and is the last pope. Frightening as this may be, things will get worse before they get better. In another part of this book you are writing, I will expand upon my prophecies all of which will come true before my son returns to earth.

A horrific number of lives and souls will be lost in the coming years. Dear son, I suggest you at this time document all the wars in the world right now. It is Heartbreaking yet I knew all of this would happen and so now you too.

Let us, you, and I, now proceed with far more details in this magnificent Book and I want you to center upon my apparitions that talk about the End of Times.

I love you ever so much my dearest son. You are protected and always in my prayers.

Your Blessed Mother Mary

Question, dear Mother Mary: If you don't mind being quantitative as I am. Could you put a numerical figure on just how many times you appeared to different children in separate places on earth to deliver your messages and your warnings?

Answer*: Oh, of course dear son, I will. You may be surprised but remember I also appeared without saying anything to anybody. It is my image of love and peace that appears to people to remind them of not only me but my messages of love, peace, sacrifice, prayer, the mass, and the powerful Rosary. These are too numerous to mention because ever so many thousands of people see my image but then my effect on their prayer life slowly fades away.*

But regarding the times in which I have spoken to selected ones of God's sacred children and have not been reported. The number you are looking for is 375 times that I have spoken to the sacred children of God. My appearance almost always produces fear among the children. Many times, they do not report what they saw because of their fear of getting into trouble with the elders. Other times elders ignore what they say thinking they are just making up fanciful stories. Even when the children describe my appearances to the parents and local elders. All along with in the contents of what I have said, the event gets tangled up and confused by people in the Church.

Many times, even the local priests and bishops accused the children of lying and this is what happened at La Salette. They reported what they saw and what was said. One of the children disappeared from the scene and the other, Maximin simply denied our encounter and said he told a falsehood. However, there are particularly important and shining examples of when things mostly go right and the legitimate appearance of mine reaches the higher authorities in the Church. But even then, due to the honest content like in Fatima, the Church hierarchy decides to hide my words of prophecy because they think it makes the Church look bad. Lastly, Garabandal, Akita and Medjugorje are good examples of things going properly and I would like you to emphasize these in this magnificent book you are writing.

People, God's sacred children must know what is coming and that things have already started that are part of the End of Times. This is not the end of the world; it is the End of Times which will be horrifically painful in so many ways that I will tell you later in this terrific book.

4

The Five Apparitions of Blessed Mother Mary

For the purposes of this booklet written when the world has entered into the End of Times, Mother Mary decided there will be a total of five of her apparitions there will be documented here. Remember Mother Mary appeared 375 times to various people on earth but for quite a number of reasons what she had to say was never distributed to all of God's sacred children as was intended. Mostly those she appeared to become very afraid and were scared to tell anyone.

These five apparitions are not in chronological sequence. The reason for this is because.

The five apparitions contained here are as follows:

1. La Salette 1846: Mother Mary discusses her sufferings in order to hold back chastisements due to our Father's sacred children's grave sins and lack of prayers. She talks about the increasing chaos and confusion leading up to World War 1 and World War 2, very prophetic and very accurate!

2. Lourdes 1858: Mother Mary wants God's children to know they can turn to their heavenly Father for healing in preparation for the coming chaos. And world wars that will start in the next 50 years and will decimate France along with many other countries.

3. Garabandal 1961: many apparitions to four children that invoked sacred transes to these children while Mother Mary was present. Known for the miracle of the host. Like all apparitions Mary's message is of hope, conversion, love, prayer, penance, and sacrifice with great emphasis on the rosary. This is the formula to end all wars. The rosary is the most powerful sacred force on earth.

4. Zeitoun 1968: This celebrates the place where the Holy Family fled to from Jerusalem due to the persecution of Herod killing all babies under age 2. Also, she wanted to demonstrate the Holy Trinity is for everyone because Zeitoun is in Islam Egypt. This is the only apparition where Mother Mary did not speak.

5. Fatima 1, 2, 3. 1917: I saved this for the last because the three secrets of Fatima especially the third deals with our modern-day times and the fact we now have already entered into the End of Times. This also includes the anti-Christian Satanic actions of the Vatican and especially Pope Francis. This is discussed with proof and great detail. Horrific to say but true. The last thing the Vatican wants is for our Heavenly Father's sacred children to have the full truth of the third secret of Fatima. That is discussed in great detail here directly from Mother Mary herself.

Mother Mary Speaks to Me About All Her Apparitions

Question: Are the apparitions on this list the only ones you appeared in or are there more? Knowing how things go, I strongly suspect there are a lot more.

Answer: *Yes, my dear son there are many more. Oh, how I wish that all the others would be made public as well. There are many reasons for the existence of the unpublished apparitions. People to whom I have spoken to get very afraid to share their experiences not only with their friends and family but especially with the Church hierarchy. The fear they will have the spotlight on them and be accused of being many negative things all of which are not true. I thank you my dear son for having the courage to publish my words of love and concern for my children on earth.*

The other reasons for apparitions not reaching the general public are the Church itself. It categorizes my appearances in such a way that most of them are automatically eliminated because priests, bishops and cardinals are very skeptical and tend to not believe what my children tell them. The other reason is what has happened with what I said to the three Shepherd children in Fatima. A lot of what I said makes the Church look bad in its own eyes. They have gone to great lengths to keep the important parts of the third secret away from God's sacred children.

My dear son, what you uncovered in your investigation is true. The Church became very dishonest and substituted the real sister Lucia with an imposter. The scientific investigations that you uncovered proved that in no way could the imposter woman in the pictures be the real sister Lucia. They went to such great lengths to keep the truth of my apparitions away from the faithful. They will pay a heavy price for that when their time comes. When we get to the section of the third secret of Fatima, I will tell you everything. Knowing that you will indeed have this published once and for all to the entire world which was my intent to begin with to have it released to the world in 1960. Because of your wonderful efforts my dear son the delay in releasing my prophecies will be only 64 years and not so very much longer.

As far as the number of prophecies and apparitions that I have appeared in that are not released to my children in numbers in many hundreds. I am incredibly sad to tell you this, but this is very real. And I cry for my children because they have been kept away from the sacred truths that they must know to help turn around the terrible path people on earth continue to be on. My warnings have been largely avoided for all the above reasons.

Remember always that the most powerful forces on earth is prayer, penance, sacrifice, and the rosary. In 1962 we came close to consecrating Russia to my Immaculate Heart to prevent so much ugly wars that have happened since then. It is said that such few people in high places can cause so many deaths among God's children.

Question: Which of these apparitions do you feel are the most important based on where we are now in human History?

Answer: *Thank you for asking me this my dear son. I think you already have a very good idea of what I'm going to say. In order they* *would be Garabandal, Our Lady of Success, our Lady of La Salette, our Lady of Lourdes, our Lady of Fatima and lastly our Lady of Akita. It is this last apparition on October 17, 1917, that is by far the most important and upsetting to people who have read it. It was necessary that my prophecy in the third secret be released to the laity within the Church immediately after my appearance. But Pope John XXIII read it and said,*

"It was not for that time."

He was wrong. It was very ready and in accordance with my will and the will of your Father and your Savior Lord Jesus Christ.

Thank you so very much my dear Blessed Mother Mary. These apparitions I will now cover in-depth according to both my research and importantly your comments to confirm or correct what is already written on what has been already published for each one.

Dear Mother Mary, His or any other comments you would like to make at this time, or would you prefer to wait until I address each of the five apparitions to discuss them than?

My dear son, yes that is wait because there are a number of things, I want to add each one of my apparitions separately.

La Salette, September 19, 1846. [2] [3]

I bring you this apparition from our Blessed Mother Mary at La Salette because of three things:

1. Our Blessed Mother Mary asked me to
2. It contains more information beyond what I have already provided regarding the actions of our Heavenly Father in answer to all of the wretched sin that is increasing day by day on earth.

---

[2] Shepherdess of La Salette with Imprimatur with Mgr. Biship of Lecce, https://www.Catholic-saints.net/prophecies/la-salette.php   La Salette Apparitions and Prophecies of Our Lady (Catholic-saints.net)

[3] Note: There are many other La Salette sites that vary in their completeness and quality. Seek them if you wish.

3. This also is theologically linked to Fatima. This contains many harsh warnings and prophies of catastrophes, suffering and wars that could have been avoided by prayer, penance, sacrifice. But people turned away from our Almighty Father

This is a direct account of Blessed Mother 's apparition where she spoke with both Melanie and Maximin a number of times. Melanie wrote down in 1878. It was published at Lecce in November 1879 and reprinted a few times. This small Booklet is now exceedingly rare but the following text excerpts is followed exactly. The account of Blessed Mother's apparition in this case is approved by the Catholic Church. Not all apparitions are but this one is in fact, most apparitions are ever approved by the Church. Lastly, remember this testimony is translated from French. Expressions and vocabulary are different than what you would expect if written in English and not translated.

Our Heavenly Fathers Love for Us and Chastisements

Dear reader, please indulge me for a moment. I have to clarify a point that comes up every time, we discuss the apparitions of Blessed Mother Mary and all her prophecies involving what is apparent punishments that come from our loving Heavenly Father.

It is an apparent contradiction of love versus punishment due to the following two thoughts:

1. Our Father in Heaven is perfect and pure love far beyond our understanding as His sacred children. Being pure love, all of His actions are always for the benefit of the spiritual health and redemption of His sacred children on earth.

2. Many times, people talk about such things as "the wrath of God," "the anger of God" and other phrases such as this.

So, the question is simply how Our Heavenly Father can be pure sacred love get what appears to be so angry at His sacred children he will punish them causing tremendous pain, agony, and death. Those two thoughts just do not fit together in our human way of thinking. So, what is the truth of things that come up in many of Blessed

Mother Mary's apparitions and her prophecies? Our Blessed Mother Mary answers this along with our Lord and Savior Jesus Christ.

March 19, 2024
Jesus Christ

Question: dear Lord Jesus, and Dear Blessed Mother Mary, how are these two apparent contradictions resolved? I think I know the answer, but all sacred children need to understand this point.

Answer: *"Boy, my dear son you are indeed a perceptive one and I love this question because it goes to the very Heart of our sacred children and their existence. The answer is what you already suspect, our Father in Heaven never gets angry in the sense that is understood by humanity on earth.*

Rather, as you already know my son, <u>your Father simply withdraws His love from His children based on the situation. So as to let the rampant sinful ugliness, which is systemic to earth so to speak and let Satan do His monstrous evil things</u>. It is this that constitutes the lessons that your Father wants all His sacred children to learn.

<u>Your Heavenly Father's love is what keeps everything on earth from falling apart.</u> This also directly involves me your Savior and our Holy Spirit. Due to Satan being the prince of the earth and all His demons, they are simply released to do what damage they can.

But also, beyond that, all the natural forces of the earth are normally held back by us well. If necessary, as in the coming "end of times" He will simply let loose these normal forces. Things like earthquakes, hurricanes, droughts and floods, volcanoes both under the sea and on land, all can be released because it is us the Trinity that does keep things as you would say glued together.

As in another prophecy of my Blessed Mother, she talks about fire from the sky and many other natural disasters. There are many asteroids beyond the planet you call Mars. They are kept in check by us the Trinity. There will come a time when we will stop doing that and many asteroids will make their way to earth and the destruction will be horrific. To get an idea of what can happen to earth just look at your moon and see all the craters brought about by asteroids. Yes, the earth was designed to heal from much of that, but this is to give you an idea of what happens if we remove our sacred protection for the planet, you call earth.

So, my dear son, your Heavenly Father never gets angry. We simply remove our ongoing protection and let the natural process of things and Satanic influence take its course. Lastly, your Blessed Mother Mary does use the language of anger. This is because this kind of vocabulary is necessary to convey in a simple and clear way how to think about God withdrawing our support for those who need to be taught a lesson. Thank you, my dear son, for asking this is a most intelligent and perceptive question."

With all this in mind, let us now proceed with the wonderful apparitions from our Blessed Mother Mary.

Blessed Mother Mary's Apparition At La Salette

On Saturday, September 19, 1846, in the afternoon, Mother Mary appeared to two shepherd children Melanie and Maximin. From this encounter Melanie writes the following:

"Maximin, do you see what is over there? Oh! My God!" At the same moment, I dropped the stick I was holding. Something inconceivably fantastic passed through me in that moment and I felt myself being drawn. I felt a profound respect, full of love, and my heartbeat faster.

I kept my eyes fixed on this light, which was static. And as if it opened up, I caught sight of another more brilliant light. This one was moving, and in this light, I saw a most beautiful lady sitting on top of our Paradise, with her head in her hands. This beautiful Lady stood up; she coolly crossed her arms while watching us. Maximin Giraud and Mélanie Calvat, reported Our Blessed Mother Mary's apparition to have occurred at La Salette-Fallavaux, France, in 1846. She said to us.

"Come, my children, fear not, I am here to PROCLAIM GREAT NEWS TO YOU."

When I was up close to the Beautiful Lady, in front of her to her right, she began to speak and from her beautiful eyes tears also started to flow.

"If my people do not wish to submit themselves, I am forced to let go of the hand of my Son. It is so heavy and weighs me down so much I can no longer keep hold of it.

"I have suffered all of the time for the rest of you! If I do not wish my Son to abandon you, I must take it upon myself to pray for this continually. And the rest of you think little of this. In vain you will pray, in vain you will act, and you will never be able to make up for the trouble I have taken over for the rest of you.

Note: understand that the beautiful love of Our Blessed Mother Mary propels her to pray for us in substitution for the prayers we ourselves should be making.

"Melanie, what I am about to tell you now will not always be a secret. You may make it public in 1858.

"The priests, ministers of my Son, the priests, by their wicked lives, by their irreverence and their impiety in the celebration of the Holy mysteries. By their love of money, their love of honors and pleasures. And the priests have become cesspools of impurity. Yes, the priests are asking vengeance, and vengeance is hanging over their heads. Woe to the priests and to those dedicated to God who by their unfaithfulness and their wicked lives are crucifying my Son again! The sins of those dedicated to God cry out towards Heaven. And call for vengeance, and now vengeance is at their door, for there is no one left to beg mercy and forgiveness for the people. There are no more generous souls; there is no one left worthy of offering a stainless sacrifice to the Eternal for the sake of the world.

"God will strike in an unprecedented way.

"Woe to the inhabitants of the earth! God will exhaust His wrath upon them, and no one will be able to escape so many afflictions together.

"The chiefs, the leaders of the people of God have neglected prayer and penance, and the devil has bedimmed their intelligence. They have become wandering stars which the old devil will drag along with

His tail to make them perish. God will allow the old serpent to cause divisions among those who reign in every society and in every family. Physical and moral agonies will be suffered. God will abandon mankind to itself and will send punishments which will follow one after the other for more than thirty-five years.

Question: Has this happened already? In What Form? If not when?

Mother Mary: *thank you for asking my son, I was referring to the early 1900s that was coming quickly upon them. France was already in turmoil and so chaos and confusion was happening increasingly in preparation for World War I and then World War II. Both of which were fought in France in one way or another. It became a terrible time of suffering in all different ways. Napoleon ran over all the land in His attempt to dominate everybody and everything and it got worse over time.*

"The priests, ministers of my Son, the priests, by their wicked lives, by their irreverence and their impiety in the celebration of the holy mysteries. By their love of money, their love of honors and pleasures, and the priests have become cesspools of impurity. Yes, the priests are certainly asking vengeance, and vengeance is hanging over their heads. Woe to the priests and to those dedicated to God who by their unfaithfulness and their wicked lives are crucifying my Son again! The sins of those dedicated to God cry out towards Heaven and call for vengeance. And now vengeance is at their door, for there is no one left to beg mercy and forgiveness for the people. There are no more generous souls; there is no one left worthy of offering a stainless sacrifice to the Eternal for the sake of the world.

"God will strike in an unprecedented way.

"Woe to the inhabitants of the earth! God will exhaust His wrath upon them, and no one will be able to escape so many afflictions together.

"The chiefs, the leaders of the people of God have neglected prayer and penance, and the devil has bedimmed their intelligence. They have become wandering stars which the old devil will drag along with

His tail to make them perish. God will allow the old serpent to cause divisions among those who reign in every society and in every family. Physical and moral agonies will be suffered. God will abandon mankind to itself and will send punishments which will follow one after the other for more than thirty-five years.

"The Society of men is on the eve of the most terrible scourges and of gravest events. Mankind must expect to be ruled with an iron rod and to drink from the chalice of the wrath of God.

Question: Dear Mother Mary, I take it then the above paragraphs are your warnings of the terrible sufferings and agonies that are coming. Because it is as if Our Father Almighty has been relegated to the background within the Hearts of the people and priests. Therefore, our Father will withdraw and let humanity take its sinful course and experience the awful consequences. Do I have this right?

Mother Mary: *Yes, my dear son you have it exactly right. <u>If there is one thing that I would love you to communicate to all others of God sacred children through your writings is that prayer is the most powerful force on earth.</u> As I have said so many times prayer, penance, sacrifice, and the rosary along with the sacraments are the road to happiness, fulfillment, and success while on the earth. You could say that doing these things is <u>the antidote of Satan</u>. In an atmosphere of prayer in love Satan can do almost nothing.*

"May the curate of my Son, Pope Pius IX never leave Rome again after 1859; may he, however, be steadfast and noble<u>, may he fight with the weapons of faith and love</u>. I will be at His side. May he be on His guard against Napoleon: he is two-faced, and when he wishes to make Himself Pope as well as Emperor, God will soon draw back from Him. He is the mastermind who, always wanting to ascend further, will fall on the sword he wished to use to force His people to be raised up.

Question: my dear Mother Mary, the above paragraph seems to have the timing of Napoleon's lifetime incorrect because he died before Pope Pius IX was in His papacy.

Answer: *"You are so right my love; my son told me how perceptive you are, and I thank you for that. The discontinuity that you observed is correct. After the death of Napoleon, the political and military situation in France remained very hostile toward the Church. Napoleon failed in becoming both Emperor and Pope and that thought lingered on for a very long time regarding uniting the political with the spiritual.*

Today as you know there are very strong tendencies in the world to do now exactly what Napoleon failed at. Many world leaders during your lifetime, like Napoleon, want to combine all countries into a one-world government and a one-world religion. This effort is gaining in ferocity with Pope Francis trying to secularize the Catholic Church that my son founded. In addition, world political leaders are now working toward a one-world government through the guidance of many worldwide organizations like NATO and the WEF, the world economic forum. These are very evil people and like other prophecies, the Satanic urges have started from the top like Pope Francis.

If they succeed in doing this it is Satan that will be installed as the worldwide leader, and he will rampage across the world subjugating everybody to worship Him and follow His Satanic laws. If you do not obey you will become a nonperson and will either, be killed or you will starve to death. You will be banned from all economic activity like purchasing food and shelter.

My personal political warning.

There is a direct linkage between our two political parties and what Napolean killed so many people for.

Democrats want complete centralized government control over every aspect of our lives.

They are going as far as to regulate what our natural gas stoves can do or not.

They want to regulate every detail of our lives including the kind of cars we drive.

They use fake science of climate change. It is completely false and a Satanic falsehood. Democrats hate our Godly inspired Constitution.

Democrats hate our Bill of Rights because it greatly limits the power of a central government Democrats adore centralized government.

Democrats reject our Almighty Father.

They preach people are nothing but an accidental pile of chemicals that started in a swamp.

The Democrat Party is nothing more than the political arm of Satan.

They hate life as created by our Father and love killing it in the womb using "women's" rights as an excuse.

They crave power and control of everyone's life.

They will stop at nothing to persecute political rivals. Look no farther than the persecution of Donald Trump.

Democrats have completely ignored the rule of law and constitutional government in order to assassinate His legal bid for the presidency.

They continually invent more and more government programs to "help the needy" and over the years this has accounted for now the vast majority of where our tax dollars go.

This is why Democrats have opened the borders of our country to the world. So, they may import new voters that will most likely vote Democrat because they are so happy to get out of their stinking countries.

Former president Democrat Barack Obama once said, he sees no reason why the United States should be any better than the rest of the world! Now Democrats are importing the rest of the world into our beloved country.

All the Democrats have one intention, increase the size of government, and buy votes so they can retain more and more political power. This is why they always increase taxes because that also forces hardworking people down the economic ladder into need for government programs. It is a vicious Satanic cycle. Lastly my dear sacred child of God <u>I say this again with a bleeding Heart, "Our Democrat party is the political arm of Satan in our country."</u>

Contrarily, Republicans believe in individual freedom for everyone, no exceptions. Freedom to choose what we wish to purchase, where we want to go and how we lead our lives. Republicans want as small of a government as possible and as much freedom as possible for all our sacred children and citizens of our country. Not much more to be said because all this is very straightforward.

Now let's go back to the sacred words of our Blessed Mother Mary:

This is why, please communicate to everybody to use <u>the most powerful weapon on earth which is sincere prayer to the holy Trinity. With enough prayer the terrible situation I just described may very well never happen.</u> But my dearest son, I am not optimistic. Due to people like the current Pope Francis who is steadfastly attempting to take the holy and sacred aspects of the Catholic Church and turn it into just other empty secular organization. As you already know my dear son, Pope Francis is indeed the Anti-Christ and everything he has been doing fits that description.

On another note, dear son, Father Malachi Martin is correct when he stated that <u>there is Satanic worship going on within the Vatican.</u> And this has been so for a long time now, but it is increasing in its intensity."

"Italy will be punished for her ambition in wanting to shake off the yoke of the Lord of Lords. And so, she will be left to fight a war; blood will flow on all sides. Churches will be locked up or desecrated. Priests and religious orders will be hunted down and made to die a cruel death. Several will abandon the faith, and a vast number of priests and members of religious orders will break away from the true religion; among these people there will even be bishops.

"May the Pope guard against the performers of miracles. For the time has come when the most astonishing wonders will take place on the earth and in the air.

"In the year 1864, Lucifer together with a large number of demons will be unloosed from hell; they will put an end to faith little

by little, even in those dedicated to God. They will blind them in such a way, that, unless they are Blessed with a special grace, these people will take on the spirit of these angels of hell. Several religious institutions will lose all faith and will lose many souls.

Question: Dear Mother Mary, how many churches are already closed in America and the rest of the world?

Answer: *thank you for asking my dear son, it is a dire situation, and it is getting worse. The short answer to your question is within the United States between 1 and 2 thousand different churches have already closed due to decreasing lack of participation from parishioners. In the rest of the world the percentage of Christian and Catholic churches that are disappearing is even worse. Across the entire world there is between 5 thousand and 10 thousand different churches that have closed in the last few decades. As time gets deeper and deeper into the End of Times these numbers will increase. To quantities that is very frightening as the Catholic Church and other Christian churches will be forced to go underground just as your lifelong friend brother Bracco has forecasted for many years.*

"Evil Booklets will be abundant on earth and the sprits of darkness will spread everywhere a universal slackening of all that concerns the service of God. They will have great power over nature. There will be Churches built to serve these spirits. People will be transported from one place to another by these evil spirits. Even priests, for they will not have been guided by the good spirit of the Gospel which is a spirit of humility, charity, and zeal for the glory of God.

On occasions, the dead and the righteous will be brought back to life. (That is to say that these dead will take on the form of righteous souls. Which had lived on earth, in order to lead men further astray. These so-called resurrected dead. Who will be nothing but the devil in this form will preach another Gospel contrary to that of the true Christ Jesus. Denying the existence of Heaven; that is also to say, the souls of the damned. All these souls will appear as if fixed to their bodies.

"Everywhere there will be extraordinary wonders, as true faith has faded, and false light brightens the people. Woe to the Princes of the Church who think only of piling riches upon riches to protect their authority and dominate with pride.

Question: Dearest Mother Mary, all this is just awful. At this point in human History can you please give us an idea of the time in which the above Satanic events will occur or have already occurred?

Answer: *My dear son, much of this has already happened since my apparition in La Salette. But the Satanic activities continue onward even until today. The Catholic Popes that have served the Church well since my prophecy above have suffered badly but this suffering is not getting the attention of the true believers in the Church.*

Your current Pope Francis will be going to Moscow sometime in the near future after this Booklet has been written. Remember Russia has not been properly consecrated. If it were the wars such as Ukraine today would never have happened. And the world would be heading toward a far more peaceful existence. Do not believe that Pope Francis will consecrate Russia while he is in Moscow. His visit there is purely political.

"The Vicar of my Son will suffer a great deal, because for a while the Church will yield to large persecution, a time of darkness and the Church will witness a frightful crisis.

"The true faith to the Lord having been forgotten, each individual will want to be on his own and be superior to people of same identity. They will abolish civil rights. As well as ecclesiastical, all order and all justice would be trampled underfoot and only homicides, hate, jealousy, falsehoods, and dissension would be seen without love for country or family.

"The Holy Father will suffer a great deal. I will be with Him until the end and receive His sacrifice. The mischievous would attempt his life several times to do harm and shorten his days but neither him nor his successor will see the triumph of the Church of God. All the civil governments will have one and the same plan, which will be

to abolish and do away with every religious principal to make way for materialism, atheism, spiritualism, and vices of all kinds.

In the year 1865, there will be desecration of holy places. In convents, the flowers of the Church will decompose, and the devil will make himself like the king of all hearts. May those in charge of religious communities be on their guard against the people they must receive. For the devil will resort to all His evil tricks to introduce sinners into religious orders, for disorder and the love of carnal pleasures will be spread all over the earth.

Note: Blessed Mother Mary said these things in the mid-1800s and now remember all the sexual scandals that have gone on recently in the Catholic Church. She knew this was coming. And it certainly has.

"France, Italy, Spain, and England will be at war. Blood will flow in the streets. Frenchman will fight Frenchman; Italian will fight Italian. A general war will follow which will be appalling. For a time, God will cease to remember France and Italy because the Gospel of Jesus Christ has been forgotten. The wicked will make use of all their evil ways. Men will kill each other; massacre each other even in their homes.

"At the first blow of His thundering sword, the mountains and all nature will tremble in terror, for the disorders and crimes of men have pierced the vault of the Heavens. Paris will burn and Marseilles will be engulfed. Several cities will be shaken down and swallowed up by earthquakes. People will believe that all is lost. Nothing will be seen but murder, nothing will be heard but the clash of arms and blasphemy.

"The righteous will suffer greatly. Their prayers, their penances and their tears will rise up to Heaven and all of God's people will beg for forgiveness and mercy and will plead for my help and intercession. And then Jesus Christ, in an act of His justice and His great mercy will command His Angels to have all His enemies put to death. Suddenly, the persecutors of the Church of Jesus Christ and all those given over to sin will perish and the earth will become desert-like.

And then peace will be made, and man will be reconciled with God. Jesus Christ will be served, worshipped, and glorified. Charity will flourish everywhere. The new kings will be the right arm of the holy Church, which will be strong, humble, and pious in its poor but fervent imitation of the virtues of Jesus Christ. The Gospel will be preached everywhere, and mankind will make great progress in its faith, for there will be unity among the workers of Jesus Christ and man will live in fear of God.

Question: Dear Mother Mary, are you referring to World War I and World War II?

Answer: *Yes, my son, you have perceived very well what I described. And as you know after those two awful wars, the peace was very short-lived because a short time later the Korean War in the Cold War became very visible and threatening. This peace among men will be short-lived. Twenty-five years of plentiful harvests will make them forget that the sins of men are the cause of all the troubles on this earth. A forerunner of the Anti-Christ, with his troops gathered from several nations, will fight against the true Christ, the only Savior of the world. He will shed much blood and will want to annihilate the worship of God to make Himself be looked upon as a God. The earth will be struck by calamities of all kinds (in addition to plague and famine which will be widespread. There will be a series of wars until the last war. Which will then be fought by the ten kings of the Anti-Christ, all of whom will have one and the same plan and will be the only rulers of the world. Before this comes to pass, there will be a kind of false peace in the world. People will think of nothing but amusement. The wicked will give themselves over to all kinds of sin. But the children of the holy Church, the children of my faith, my true followers, they will grow in their love for God and in all the virtues most precious to me. Blessed are the souls humbly guided by the Holy Spirit! I shall fight at their side until they reach a fullness of years.*

Nature is asking for vengeance because of man, and she trembles with dread at what must happen to the earth stained with crime.

Tremble, earth, and you who proclaim yourselves as serving Jesus Christ and who, on the inside, only adore yourselves. Tremble, for God will hand you over to His enemy, because the holy places are in a state of corruption. Many convents are no longer houses of God, but the grazing-grounds of Asmodeus and His like. It will be during this time that the Anti-Christ will be born of a Hebrew nun, a false virgin who will communicate with the old serpent, the master of impurity, His Father will be. At birth, he will spew out blasphemy; he will have teeth, in a word; he will be the devil incarnate. He will scream horribly; he will perform wonders; he will feed on nothing but impurity. He will have brothers who, although not devils incarnate like Him, will be children of evil. At the age of twelve, they will draw attention upon themselves by the gallant victories they will have won; soon they will each lead armies, aided by the legions of hell.

The seasons will be altered, the earth will produce nothing but bad fruit, the stars will lose their regular motion, and the moon will only reflect a faint reddish glow. Water and fire will give the earth's globe convulsions and terrible earthquakes which will swallow up mountains, cities, etc... Rome will lose the faith and become the seat of the Anti-Christ. The demons of the air together with the Anti-Christ will perform great wonders on earth and in the atmosphere, and men will become more and more perverted. God will take care of His faithful servants and men of goodwill. The Gospel will be preached everywhere, and all peoples of all nations will get to know the truth.

"I make an urgent appeal to the earth. I call on the true disciples of the living God who reigns in Heaven. I call on the true followers of Christ made man, the only true Savior of men. I call on my children, the true faithful. Those who have given themselves to me so that I may lead them to my divine Son. Those whom I carry in my arms, so to speak, those who have lived on my spirit. Finally, I call on the Apostles of the Last Days. The faithful disciples of Jesus Christ. Who have lived in scorn for the world and for themselves, in poverty and in humility, in scorn and in silence, in prayer and in

mortification, in chastity and in union with God. In suffering and unknown to the world. It is time they came out and filled the world with light. Go and reveal yourselves to be my cherished children. I am at your side and within you, provided that your faith is the light which shines upon you in these unhappy days. May your zeal make you famished for the glory and the honor of Jesus Christ. Fight, children of light, you, the few who can see. For now, is the time of all times, the end of all ends.

The Church will be in eclipse; the world will be in dismay. But now Enoch and Eli will come, filled with the Spirit of God. They will preach with the might of God, and men of goodwill will believe in God, and many souls will be comforted. They will make great steps forward through the virtue of the Holy Spirit and will condemn the devilish lapses of the Anti-Christ. Woe to the inhabitants of the earth! There will be bloody wars and famines, plagues, and infectious diseases. It will rain with a fearful hail of animals.

There will be thunderstorms which will shake cities, earthquakes which will swallow up countries. Voices will be heard in the air. Men will beat their heads against walls, call for their death, and on another side, death will be their torment. Blood will flow on all sides. Who will be the victor if God does not shorten the length of the test? All the blood, the tears, and prayers of the righteous, God will relent. Enoch and Eli will be put to death. Pagan Rome will disappear. The fire of Heaven will fall and consume three cities. All the universes will be struck with terror, and many will let themselves be lead astray because they have not worshipped the true Christ who lives among them. It is time; the sun is darkening; only faith will survive.

Now is the time; the abyss is opening. Here is the King of Kings of darkness; here is the Beast with His subjects, calling Himself the Savior of the world. He will rise proudly into the air to go to Heaven. He will be Mothered by the breath of the Archangel Saint Michael. He will fall! And the earth, which will have been in a continuous series of evolutions for three days, will open up its fiery bowels. And he will have plunged for all eternity with all His followers into the everlasting chasms of hell. And then water and fire will purge the earth and consume all the works of men's pride, and all will be renewed. God will be served and glorified."

Then the Holy Virgin gave me, also in French, THE RULE OF A NEW RELIGIOUS ORDER. When She had given me the Rule of this new religious Order, the Holy Virgin continued the speech in the same manner:

If they convert, the stones and rocks will change into wheat, and potatoes will be found sown in the earth. Do you say your prayers properly, my children?" We both told a falsehood: "Oh! No, Madame, not so much. Oh! My children, you must tell them morning and evening. When you can do no more, say a Pater and an Ave Maria; and when you have the time to do better, you will say more. Only a few old women go to Mass. In the summer, the rest work all day Sunday and, in the winter, when they are at a loose end, they only go to Mass to make fun of religion. During Lent, they go to the butchers like hungry dogs.

Have you ever seen any spoilt wheat, my children?"

We both answered: "Oh no, Madame."

The Holy Virgin turned to Maximin, saying:

But you, my child, you must have seen some once near le 'Coin,' with your Father. The farmer said to your Father: 'Come and see how my wheat's gone bad!' You went to see. Your Father took two or three ears in His hand, rubbed them, and they fell to dust. Then, on your way back, when you were no more than half an hour away from Corps, your Father gave you a piece of bread, and said: 'Take it, eat it while you can, my son, for I don't know who will be eating anything next year if the wheat is spoiled like that!'"

The Most Holy Virgin brought her speech to an end in French. The most beautiful Lady crossed the stream. After two more steps, without turning back towards us following Her (for we were drawn to her by her brilliance, her kindness which elated me and melted my heart), she repeated to us:

"AND SO, MY CHILDREN, YOU WILL PASS THIS ON TO ALL MY PEOPLE"

Summary Comments About La Salette

Thank you, my dear son, for letting me comment upon my apparitions at La Salette. In many ways news very sad for me to tell both children what I had to say. My message was so much the same for them as the other apparitions that I mentioned to you earlier that were never made public by those to whom I spoke. However, I am so happy that both Malanie and Maximin did write extensively about what I said. What they said is very correct especially considering all the translator help and bias that was inserted into their words that described more simply what it was I told them.

In many cases dear son my message is the same, due to Satan and His demons your Father's sacred children fall into sin from Satanic temptations that are disguised by Him as something good. One thing I want to make note of. It seems that the more sophisticated the people are the more likely they are to fall into grave sin promoted by Satan. It is very beautiful to speak with children that believe in their Heavenly Father and their Lord and Savior my son.

So, the only thing I have left to say regarding my apparition here is to be diligent in prayer. Pray every day at least morning and evening. Make sacrifices in the name of my Immaculate Heart, do penance as you understand it to be and attend holy mass every week if you can and receive the holy sacraments. A lot of people refer to these as putting on your sacred armor. Although this is true, I prefer to think of these as acts of love for Almighty God and not something warlike. But that is just my personal preference. Thank you my dear son and I know we will continue with the others of my apparitions in your marvelous Booklet that is how starting to take form.

I love you,

Your Blessed Mother Mary

Both Melanie and Maximin were simple shepherd children when all of this happened to them. We do not know exactly when each of them wrote the following text about Our Blessed Mother Mary. However, looking at the English language presented below it is obvious they both had a lot of linguistic and vocabulary help in their writing. Additionally, it is unknowable that this point just how much their original thoughts were amplified to make more exciting reading.

Blessed Mother Mary: *Yes, again my son you are correct. But what is presented below about me from both children although exaggerated have the essential ideas intact.*

Maximin Describes Our Blessed Mother Mary

The Most Holy Virgin was tall and well-proportioned. She seemed so light that a mere breath could have stirred Her, yet She was motionless and perfectly balanced. Her face was majestic, imposing, but not imposing in the manner of the Lords here below. She compelled a respectful fear. At the same time, as Her Majesty compelled respect mingled with love, She drew me to Her. Her gaze was soft and penetrating. Her eyes seemed to speak to mine, but the conversation came out of a deep and vivid feeling of love for this ravishing beauty who was liquefying me. The softness of Her gaze, Her air of incomprehensible goodness made me understand and feel she was drawing me to Her and wanted to give Herself. It was an expression of love which cannot be expressed with the tongue of the flesh, nor with the letters of the alphabet.

The clothing of the Most Holy Virgin was silver white and quite brilliant. It was quite intangible. It was made up of light and glory, sparkling and dazzling. There is no expression nor comparison to be found on earth.

The Holy Virgin was all beauty and all love; the sight of Her overwhelmed me. In her finery as in Her person, everything radiated the majesty, the splendor, the magnificence of a Queen beyond compare. She seemed as white, Immaculate, crystallized, dazzling, Heavenly, fresh, and new as a Virgin. The word LOVE seemed to slip from Her pure and silvery lips. She appeared to me like a good Mother, full of kindness, amiability, of love for us, of compassion and mercy.

The crown of roses which She placed on Her head was so beautiful, so brilliant, that it defies imagination. The different colored roses were not of this earth; it was a joining together of flowers which crowned the head of the Most Holy Virgin. But the roses kept changing and replacing each other, and then, from the Heart of each rose, there shone a beautiful entrancing light, which gave the roses a shimmering beauty. From the crown of roses there seemed to arise golden branches and a number of little flowers mingled with the shining ones. The whole thing formed a most beautiful diadem, which alone shone brighter than our earth's sun.

The Holy Virgin had a most pretty cross hanging round Her neck. This cross seemed golden, (golden rather than gold-plated, for I have sometimes seen objects which were golden with varying shades of gold, which had a much more beautiful effect on my eyes than simple gold-plate). On this shining, beautiful cross, there was a Christ; it was Our Lord on the Cross. Near both ends of the cross there was a hammer, and at the other end, a pair of tongs. The Christ was skin-colored, but He shone dazzlingly; and the light shone forth from His holy body seemed like brightly shining darts which pierced my Heart with the desire to melt inside Him. At times, the Christ appeared to be dead. His head was bent forward, and His body seemed to give way, as if about to fall, had He not been held back by the nails which held Him to the Cross.

I felt deep compassion. And would have liked to tell His unknown love to the whole world. And to let seep into mortal souls the most heartfelt love and gratitude towards a God who had no need whatsoever of us to be everything He is, was and always will be. And yet, O love men cannot understand, He made Himself man, and wanted to die for us. Yes, die, so as to better inscribe in our souls and in our memory, the passionate love He has for us! Oh, how wretched am I to find myself so poor in my expression of the love of our good Savior for us! But, in another way, how happy we are to be able to feel more deeply that which we cannot express!

At other times, the Christ appeared to be alive. His head was erect, His eyes open, and He seemed to be on the cross of His own accord. At times too, He appeared to speak: He seemed to show He was on the cross for our sake, out of love for us, to draw us to His love, and He always has more love to give us. His love in the beginning and in the year 33 is always that of today and will be forever more.

The Holy Virgin was crying nearly the whole time she was speaking to me. Her tears flowed gently, one by one, down to her knees, then, like sparks of light, they disappeared. They were glittering and full of love. I would have liked to comfort Her and stop Her tears. But it seemed to me She needed the tears to show better Her love forgotten by men. I would have liked to throw myself into Her arms and say to Her:

"My kind Mother do not cry! I want to love you for all men on earth." But she seemed to be saying to me:

"There are so many who know me not!"

I was in between life and death, and on one side, I saw so much desire by this Mother to be loved, and on another side, so much cold and indifference... Oh! My Mother, most beautiful and lovable Mother, my love, Heart of my Heart!

The tears of our sweet Mother, far from lessening her air of majesty, of a Queen and a Mistress. It seemed, on the contrary, to embellish Her, to make Her more beautiful. Even more powerful, more filled with love, more maternal, more ravishing, and I could have wiped away Her tears which made my heart leap with compassion and love. To see a mother cry, and such a mother, without doing everything possible to comfort her and change her grief to joy, is that possible? Oh! Mother, who is more than good; you have been formed with all the prerogatives God is able to make. You have married the power of God, so to speak; you are good, and more, you are good with the goodness of God Himself. God has extended Himself by making you His terrestrial and celestial masterpiece.

Note: There are more descriptions of Blessed Mary. Go to the website in the footnote 1 and 2. Also, my personal belief that due to the very articulate words in English, Maximin must have had help in His descriptions. The descriptions are too eloquent to be directly from a simple shepherd boy in France at that time in History. Like so many other aspirations, lots of unknown people stick their well-intended fingers into the pie so to speak.

On this point Mother Mary said to me: ***Yes, my dear son, I think he had too much help and some of the ideas originated in the translator's mind and not His. But it is generally accurate.***

Additional words of Melanie:

"The great chastisement will come, because men will not be converted; yet it is only their conversion that can hinder these scourges. God will begin to strike men by inflicting lighter punishments in order to open their eyes; then He will stop or may repeat His former warnings to give place for repentance. But sinners will not avail themselves of these opportunities; He will, in consequence, send more severe castigations, anxious to move sinners to repentance, but all in vain. Finally, the obduracy of sinners shall draw upon their heads the greatest and most terrible calamities.

"We are all guilty! Penance is not done, and sin increases daily. Those who should come forward to do good are retained by fear. Evil is great. A moderate punishment serves only to irritate the spirits, because they view all things with human eyes. God could work a miracle to convert and change the aspect of the earth without chastisement. God will work a miracle; it will be a stroke of His mercy; but after the wicked shall have inebriated themselves with blood, the scourge shall arrive.

"What countries shall be preserved from such calamities? Where shall we go for refuge? I, in my turn, shall ask, what is the country that observes the commandments of God? What country is not influenced by human fear where the interest of the Church and the glory of God are at stake? (Ah, indeed! What country, what nation upon earth?) On behalf of my Superior and myself, I have often asked myself where we could go for refuge, had we the means for the journey. Where do we go for our subsistence, on condition no person was to know it? But I renounce these useless thoughts. We are very guilty! In consequence of this, it is necessary that a very great and terrible scourge should come to revive our faith, and to restore to us our very reason, which we have almost entirely lost.

Wicked men are devoured by a thirst for exercising their cruelty; but when they shall have reached the uttermost point of barbarity,

God Himself shall extend His hand to stop them. And very soon after, a complete change shall be affected in all surviving persons. Then they will sing the Deum Landaus with the liveliest gratitude and love. The Virgin Mary, our Mother, shall be our liferentrix. Peace shall reign, and the charity of Jesus Christ shall unite all Hearts...Let us pray; let us pray. God does not wish to chastise us severely. He speaks to us in so many, so many ways to make us return to Him. How long shall we remain stubborn? Let us pray, let us pray; let us never cease praying and doing penance. Let us pray for our Holy Father the Pope, the only light for the faithful in these times of darkness. O yes, let us by all means prays much. Let us pray to sweet, good, merciful Virgin Mary; for we stand in great need of her powerful hands over our heads."

Lourdes [4]

Miraculous Holy Events Occur

Authors note: the chronology of events regarding Saint Bernadette and her companions is too precise to be written by a 14-year-old uneducated girl. To me at least she must have had a lot of help from adults to create the accounts of the apparitions of our Blessed Mother Mary. This certainly this is not to say adults modified the content of Saint Bernadette's experiences to make it sound better. I know this story is completely true. How do I know this? Because I truly am the Anointed Messenger of our Heavenly Father and Blessed Mother Mary personally told me these accounts are true and correct.

I should comment that of all the apparitions of our Blessed Mother Mary she never chooses anybody of wealth vast education. I understand why. In my opinion, it is because people of means have walked away from the purity of a simple life. Which is something Our Blessed Mother Mary feels is necessary to deliver her messages in a pure way without tainting them from the things of this world.

---

[4]   https://theCatholictravelguide.com/destinations/france/lourdes-france-lady-lourdes-site-healing-hope/

On February 11th, 1858, to July 16th our Blessed Mother Mary appeared to 14-year-old Bernadette Soubirous. In total our Blessed Mother appeared to her 18 separate times. Like me your author, Bernadette suffered from lifelong asthma. Her family was very poor.

On February 11, 1858, the day of the first apparition Bernadette and her sister Toinette, and a friend of theirs, Jeanne, were out searching for firewood to make dinner. Bernadette's companions crossed the river, but she did not because of the ice-cold water and her asthma. Suddenly Bernadette heard a sound like a woosh. She turned around and looked up into the grotto which was next to the river. She then saw that The Cave was filled with golden light.

When she looked up, she saw a lady of great beauty wearing a white robe with a blue sash and a veil over her head with a rosary in her hands. There were yellow flowers at her feet. Then the beautiful lady made the sign of the cross with the hand that was holding the rosary. Both the lady and Bernadette said the rosary together. When they finished their prayers, the beautiful lady disappeared.

As always seems to be the case, Bernadette did not want to tell her mother or father of what happened, but her sister spilled the beans and told her mother everything. Upon hearing this the mother told Bernadette those were just illusions and forbid her from going back to the grotto.

The 2nd apparition, three days later the girls went back to the grotto with holy water. They were told if they sprinkled holy water on the lady, if the lady was good then no harm done if the lady was evil, it would force her to disappear. Bernadette sprinkles the water on the ground at her feet and Blessed Mother Mary smiled. On February 18th the 3rd apparition took place. The next time the three girls went to the grotto Bernadette had a pencil and paper so as to write down anything our Blessed Mother Mary would tell them. When Mother Mary arrived, she told the girls, "There is no need me to write down what I have to say to you. Will you be so kind as to come here every day for 15 days? I do not promise to make you happy in this life, but in the next."

The first statement: A neighbor suggested she take a paper and pencil to write down the lady's name (although Bernadette could barely read or write). Bernadette held out a sheet of paper and a pencil so she might write down her name, but the Lady said: "what I have to say to you does not have to be written down ". This was the first statement Mother Mary made that day.

The second statement of the Virgin Mary was: "Would you do me the kindness of coming here for 15 days?" Bernadette was overwhelmed. It was the first time anyone addressed her in a formal way. Bernadette described these words by saying the Virgin looked at her "as one person looks at another person."

The third statement of the Virgin was: "I do not promise to make you happy in this world but in the next."

The 4th apparition, a Friday. Bernadette's parents and a few friends went to the grotto this time. When Bernadette started to pray the rosary, the other people noticed her face became illuminated.

The 5th apparition on, Blessed Mother Mary taught Bernadette a prayer she recited every day for the rest of her life. But Bernadette never revealed the prayer to anyone else. Also, Mother Mary told her to always bring a candle.

The 6th apparition on: Bernadette's experience with Mother Mary caused a sensation in the community and many people started to accompany her to the grotto. And is usual with Mother Mary's apparitions the townspeople became afraid and started to concentrate on the dangers of too many people gathering at the grotto. So, the officials forbid Bernadette from going to the grotto. I like Bernadette very much! Because she told the people she cannot obey and will go to the grotto to see the beautiful lady.

The ninth apparition was really the culmination of the apparitions here at Lourdes, the Lady asked Bernadette to scrape the ground at the back of this "pigs' shelter," saying to her: "Go to the spring, drink of it and wash yourself there ". She moved on her knees to the back of the Grotto, kissed the dirty disgusting ground and ate some bitter grass. She scraped the ground three times trying to drink the muddy water, then smeared mud on her face. Then she turned to the crowd with her hands apart. There was only a little muddy water to begin with for Bernadette to drink, then little by little it became clear running water. The miraculous spring was finally revealed, and has continued to flow ever since, providing water for the physical healing of some, and spiritual healing for millions. [5]

Then, during the thirteenth apparition, March 25, 1858, the crowd became larger and larger. The Lady told her: "Go and tell the priests that people are to come here in procession and to build a chapel here." Bernadette spoke of this to Fr. Peyramale, the Parish Priest of Lourdes.

He wanted to know only one thing: the Lady's name. He demanded another test; to see the wild rosebush flower at the Grotto in the middle of winter. Three times Bernadette asked the question. On the fourth request, the Lady responded in dialect "Que soy era Immaculada Conception." ("I am the Immaculate Conception ").

With these words the Mother of God confirmed what Pope Pius IX proclaimed as the dogma of the Immaculate Conception four years earlier in 1854. Bernadette, who never heard of this title, didn't understand the meaning of these words, but went to the priest to tell Him the Lady's name. He knew immediately that it was the Mother

[5]   https://theCatholictravelguide.com/destinations/france/lourdes-france-lady-lourdes-site-healing-hope

of God, and the Bishop of Tarbes, Monseigneur Laurence, confirmed this.

The Immaculate Conception is, as the Church teaches, "Mary, conceived without sin, thanks to the merits of the Cross of Christ."

We celebrate the Feast of Our Lady of Lourdes on February 11.

The lady also told Bernadette to dig in the ground at a certain spot and to drink from the small spring of water that began to bubble up. Almost immediately, cures were reported from the water. Today thousands of gallons of water gush from the source of the spring, and pilgrims are able to bathe in it. Countless purported miracle cures have been documented there, from the healing of nervous disorders and cancers to cases of paralysis and even of blindness. [6]

A Summary of What Blessed Mother Mary Said: [7]

- Feb 18, 1858 (Ash Wednesday) It is not necessary [to write down my name]. Would you be kind enough to come here for 15 days? I do not promise to make you happy in this world, but in the next.
- Feb 21, 1858 (Sorrowful tone of voice) Pray for sinners.
- Feb 24, 1858 Penance! Penance! Penance! Pray to God for sinners.
- Feb 25, 1858 Go, drink of the spring, and wash yourself there. You will eat the grass that is there.
- Feb 27, 1858 Penance! Penance! Penance! Pray to God for sinners. Go, kiss the ground for the conversion of sinners. Go and tell the priests to have a chapel built here.
- Feb 28, 1858 Penance! Penance! Penance! Pray to God for sinners. Go, kiss the ground for the conversion of sinners.
- March 2, 1858 Go, tell the priests to bring people here in procession and have a Chapel built here.

---

[6] https://en.wikipedia.org/wiki/Lourdes

[7] https://en.wikipedia.org/wiki/Lourdes

• March 25, 1858 I am the Immaculate Conception. [8]

Question: Dear Mother Mary when I did some research on Lourdes, I saw a lot of commercialization surrounding the grotto and the Chapel you wanted to be built. It seems as if a lot of money changes hands for various trinkets and the holy water can be for sale. I cannot help but feel like this completely cheapens Lourdes and removes the sacred focus of what it should be. What are your feelings dear Mother?

Answer: *I understand completely my son. They have built fancy monuments for this that and the other thing. And you are correct it is become very commercialized selling the water that is intended to be free for all of God's sacred children. As you know there are now vacation packages to bring tourists to this holy site. I would rather have all the people come no matter what the reason is and if money changes hands, I will just refer to that as necessary commerce to help the poor people in Lourdes.*

Question: in none of the accounts regarding St. Bernadette I never saw any comment regarding who actually saw you and heard you speak. I am assuming it is only Bernadette just like Garabandal. Is that right?

Answer: *yes, my son it is only Bernadette that heard my voice. I must point out with that she was very diligent in accounting for everything that I said. She was only semi-literate, and she needed help from various adults to write down what she wanted to say. The accounts are quite accurate.*

Question: Regarding the sacred healing that takes place through the means of the holy water in the grotto. I know not everyone gets healed and I think I know the answer but could you dear Mother clarify how it is some people are healed and others are not?

---

[8] IBID

Answer: as you know my dear son everything is always up to your Heavenly Father. It is always His will that will be done like the prayer "Our Father." Just like in your case my son, your Father's will be that you be healed from the terminal cancer you had years ago. Because of this it was also His will that you become His Anointed Messenger. And bring all of these magnificent understandings of creation, of our Heavenly Father. And other most important descriptions of the way all of creation works together for the benefit of all your Father's sacred children.

Also, it is His will that you be able to speak with the Trinity and me at any time you wish. So as to bring to His sacred children pure and perfect understandings of their existence and all of creation. You have done marvelously well, and I know you will continue. The entire Holy Family loves you for this so very much.

Question: besides bringing healing and hope to so many of God's sacred children through the holy water of Lourdes, Are there any other purposes or goals of your apparition at Lourdes?

Answer: that certainly is the main reason for my apparition at Lourdes. But in addition to that, Lourdes like other places I have appeared, brings together people of faith and that strengthens their faith remarkably. Also, my dear son, for those people who do not believe or are borderline believers. They will move closer to their Almighty Father in Heaven after being exposed to the stories of healings and even knowing a person that was healed. The Catholic Church calls this outreach, and it is a very good and holy thing.

Question: dear Blessed Mother somehow, I think I am missing something and what I write about Lourdes. Is there something I missed you would like to include in this booklet?

Answer: My dear son, as always you have covered the topic very well. There is nothing more than I can add to what you have already written for God's sacred children. I know you plan on adding additional apparitions with small descriptions which I think is wonderful. This will stir God's sacred children's curiosity to explore other instances of where I appeared and why. I thank you deeply for that.

Garabandal

The Multiple Apparitions of Blessed Mother Mary

In the village of San Sebastian de Garabandal in Spain, from June 18, 1961, through 1965 our Blessed Mother Mary appeared in many multiple apparitions to four young girls. She brought messages of hope, conversion, and love. She also brought prophecies that surrounded the coming End of Times. Their names are Mari Loli Mezon, Jacinta González, Mari Cruz González, Maria "Conchita" Concepción. They witnessed our Blessed Mother Mary when they were in a state of ecstasy. They would always fall into this ecstasy trance before Mother Mary would appear at the same place near the village.

But before the first apparition of our Blessed Mother the four girls witnessed an angel that appeared to them over a few days. It was the Archangel Michael. On June 1, 1961, the angel announced the appearance of our Blessed Mother Mary tomorrow. Later the Virgin Mary with the child Jesus did indeed appear before them marking the beginning of a series multiple of apparitions. Our Blessed Mother Mary appeared hundreds of times to the girls in the following years.

The Girls State of Ecstasy.

When the young girls beheld their Mother, they promptly knelt oblivious to the pain of their striking the rough stones. Yet thorough medical examinations revealed no injuries to their knees. Their faces transformed in an instant entirely engrossed in divine ecstasy. Various tests were conducted on them during these raptures, and they showed no reactions to pinches, burns, or blows. Attempts to disrupt their trance were futile. Bright lights were shown into their eyes, but they displayed no discomfort. Lights that under normal circumstances could cause permanent eye damage yet their eyes remained wide open revealing a gaze of pure intense joy. These ecstatic moments varied in length with the girls often in seemingly uncomfortable positions with heads tilted back, eyes gazing Heavenward kneeling on Rocky and uneven ground. Many esteemed doctors examined the events and observed the girls during the apparitions. After extensive study, a pediatric specialist confirmed the girls always exhibited absolute normality.

Their ecstasies did not match any known psychological or physiological phenomenon. Dr. Rickard Puncher now a renowned neuropsychologist from Barcelona stated based with such manifestations for a doctor to provide a purely natural explanation.

The Powder Compact Story

After a short time, the people in the village and onlookers would give the girls small religious objects for Mother Mary to kiss for them. If the girls were not present people would leave their religious objects on the tables at the site of the apparition. There was no way the girls would know to which person each object belonged to. But during their ecstasy with their heads always turned upward to Heaven they returned each object to its owner with no mistakes for the thousands of items left by the people. These religious items included rosaries, medals, and wedding rings. The girls guided by our Blessed Mother Mary never a mistake in their returns to all the different owners.

One time, the girls found a powder compact left from an onlooker. The girls were hesitant to give a secular object to Our Blessed Mother Mary. However, when Mother Mary appeared, the first thing she asked to kiss was the powder compact. It turns out during the Spanish Civil War that same compact was used to deliver Holy Eucharist to prisoners who were waiting to be executed. It is obvious that somehow Our Blessed Mother Mary even knows such details like this. Within the spiritual realm Our Blessed Mother lives in, there are no secrets, and everything is transparent. So, if it is very normal for our Blessed Mother to know perfectly who the owner is for each object, they wanted her to kiss them.

Note: In my other Booklet titled "God's Grand Design of All Creation for Your Redemption" I

explain Our lord and savior Jesus Christ told me there are NO secrets in the spiritual realm including the Heavenly Kingdom. This Booklet is the one Our Heavenly Father asked me to write about three years ago and now on Amazon etc. for the past 10 months. Mother Mary lives in the spiritual realm, and this is why she knows the ownership of all the items she kissed for them.

Many People Were Skeptical of What They Saw.

During the apparitions of the Virgin Mary at Garabandal many were skeptical regarding what they saw when the four girls were receiving invisible communion. The four girls wanted a sign for the non-believers, so they asked for a miracle. On June 22, 1962, St. Michael announced to Conchita he would visibly give communion. Although he previously brought communion to the girls the host had never been visible. Now one time the host would be visible.

The real Picture of the visible host after it instantly appeared on Conchita's tongue.

The Virgin Mary revealed to Conchita that the small miracle of the visible host would take place on July 18. Despite the parish priest's restriction, the news spread, and many pilgrims arrived at Garabandal that day. In front of a crowd a white host miraculously appeared on Conchita's tongue, an event that was also captured on film. A witness Pepe Diaz detailed the event emphasizing the host instantaneously appeared without any movement from Conchita. A picture exists of her tongue with the host on it that appeared out of nowhere. This was truly a miracle.

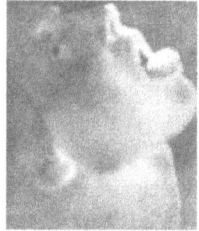

The Vatican Chose to Disbelieve Our Blessed Mother Mary's Apparitions at Garabandal

Unfortunately, but quite common within the Catholic Church, the local diocese of Santander took a negative viewpoint of all that has happened supernaturally. But the local priest Father Jose Luis Saavedra found that the investigation of the visions did not follow standard normality of impartiality. The original investigation seemed determined to discredit the visions of the four children.

"While it seemed very clear to the onlookers in Garabandal that something otherworldly was happening, the local diocese of Santander took a terribly negative approach to the events. Fr. Jose Luis Saavedra, a priest of the order of the Home of the Mother, has done His doctoral dissertation on the apparitions in Garabandal. He found that the investigation of the visions conducted by the local diocese did not follow standard norms of impartiality. The original "investigation" seemed intent on discrediting the visions out of fear of possible negative repercussions for the Church.

Then, sensationally, in May 1983, Dr. Luis Morales Noriega, the medical expert for the diocesan investigation, retracted His previously negative opinion and acknowledged the authenticity of the apparitions. To everyone's surprise, after years of negativity from the local ecclesiastical authorities, Dr Morales stated his new positive declaration was made with the permission of the bishop of Santander." [9]

Personally, I find the Catholic Church thinks backwards when it comes to the beautiful outreach of the divine to our holy Father 's sacred children on earth. We see today, and it takes the Church years upon years to certify the validity of miracles, while the faithful know what a miracle is and not without the help of the Church.

In my opinion, the Catholic Church didn't want to acknowledge or certify the validity of the miracles at Garabandal due to Our Blessed Mother Mary's prophecy the last pope will be the 112th Pope. And he would be the anti-Christ. That would be our current Pope today, Pope Francis.

Our Blessed Mary's prophecies in 1961 – 1965 include:

1.   First as always, our Blessed Mother Mary's message is of hope, conversion, and love. Additionally, she always emphasizes praying the rosary. We are to lead a life of prayer and sacrifice and be witnesses to the Gospel.

2.   There will be a period of tribulation for the world which is a warning to all humanity simultaneously. Within one year of the warning a miracle will occur in Garibaldian which will leave a visible sign for all to see. Question: Dearest Mother Mary, as this is written is now about 60 years since your apparitions in Garabandal. Is there anything now dear Mother you would like to say regarding the tribulation and the visible sign in Garabandal?

     Answer: yes, my son a few things have changed and as always thank you for asking such good questions. The situation on earth as you know is a fluid one that many times

---

[9] Garabandal: Are the Prophecies About to be Fulfilled? - Catholic Stand
https://Catholicstand.com/garabandal-are-the-prophecies-about-to-be-fulfilled/

changes like the winds. With this the warning miracle in Guerra bond L has been postponed because of an ensuing increase in Christian faith coming from of unexpected sources like Russia. The people there are more and more rejecting the government crackdowns on faith much like it was during the times of Rome when my son was crucified.

The tribulation will still occur. Sadly, because on the whole the earth is still disintegrating with Satan influence and there will be a last gasp of worldwide wars, multiple wars that are not too far off. The Russian leadership still wishes to reconstruct what was known as the Soviet Union. The current leader is becoming more and more mentally ill, and he poses a danger to the entire world. Your current leadership in our blessed United States has been doing everything it can to destroy your country. And turn it into a weakened state subject to the implementation of a one-world government and with Pope Francis a one-world religion. All of this will be led by the Anti-Christ Satan Himself.

But remember my dearest son the timing on this is not fixed and is somewhat fluid. However, my dear son I will tell you that this will happen in your later years on earth. The holy booklets that you are writing, dear son, as you recently wrote, will indeed become sacred Scripture for the generations to come. So, they will learn many more wonderful details about their existential existence, there holy Father in Heaven, and the Trinity and precisely how all existence has been designed as you have said for their redemption. Thank you, dear son I love you so much.

3. Following the miracle if humanity still fails to turn to Almighty God there will be fearful chastisement on a global scale.

    Question: can you please outline some more detail about what form the chastisement in the world will be like?

    Answer: As said in other places, it will be fire from the skies, earthquakes, wars, social unrest, economic breakdowns that will cause much hunger and suffering, lawlessness and a fundamental breakdown of all human existence. It hurts me to say this my son, but this will happen. As you have already said, it is starting to happen now and will get worse with time.

4. Our Lady additionally revealed that the warning would occur at a time when Russia will suddenly and unexpectedly over run a great part of the free world. Russia has already overrun a large country in Eastern Europe, Ukraine.

5. Lady's apparitions included other supernatural events such as levitation is, reading of thoughts, insensitivity to pain, healings, and supernatural knowledge. Doctors and psychiatrists testified to an enormous multitude of such events in their writings. [10]

6. **Question**: dear Mother is there any details you would like to add to this item?

    Answer*: Yes, there were a few instances of levitation with the four girls. Although, they did not want to mention this much because they felt people would never believe it and they were shy as I said before. It is proven the girls were very insensitive during their ecstasy to any outside influence of pain on their bodies and their attention on me. There supernatural knowledge refers to what I have told them, and you are documenting for all to see.*

7. On July 4, 1961, the Virgin Mary delivered a message to the girls, which was made public on October 18. It urged penance, visits to the Blessed sacrament and leading a righteous life, otherwise a significant punishment would befall humanity.

8. A second message was revealed by St. Michael the Archangel on behalf of the virgin on June 18, 1965.

[10] Garabandal: Are the Prophecies About to be Fulfilled? - Catholic Stand
https://Catholicstand.com/garabandal-are-the-prophecies-about-to-be-fulfilled/

9. **Question**: I have not uncovered what St. Michael the ark angel revealed on your behalf. Could you please reveal that now?

   Answer: *yes, he reiterated the very much important need for what I have always said about penance, sacrifice, prayer, and saying the rosary with receiving the sacraments frequently.*

10. October 18, 1961: We must make many sacrifices, perform much penance, and visit the Blessed Sacrament frequently. But first we must lead good lives. If we do not a chastisement will befall us. The cup is already filling up and if we do not change, a great chastisement will come upon us." (In other words, our Heavenly Father is becoming increasingly concerned and is losing His patients with us His children.)

11. "Even less importance is being given to the holy Eucharist. We should turn the wrath of God away from us by our own efforts. If you ask His forgiveness with a sincere Heart, he will party you."

12. June 18, 1965, as my 18 October message has not been compiled with in as it has not been seen made known to the world, I am telling you that this is the last one. Previously the cup was filing; now it is brimming over. <u>Many cardinals, bishops, and priests are following the road to perdition, and with them they are taking many more souls</u>.

   Question: *My dearest Mother Mary, it bothers me greatly regarding the previous prophecy that says cardinals, bishops, and priests following the road to perdition are taking many souls with them. Will our loving Father in Heaven punish some of His sacred children because of believing in what the Church tells them?*

   Answer: *my dear son again you are ever so perceptive in everything. I love you for this because you always want to dig for the truth of things. Also, I am happy that it bothers you because this shows your great love for others of God sacred children. <u>None of God's sacred children, not even one will be excluded from Heaven because they believed a wayward Church official.</u>*

It is the priests, the bishops and the Cardinals that will be greatly punished for misrepresenting my Son's message to the world. As you know my dear son there are many priests in hell along with cardinals and yes even Popes. This will be shocking to many people, but your loving Father requires honesty and close adherence to His loving laws of existence.

And like anyone else, those who believed the Church and were led astray will be judged by the very same three laws that you have so faithfully published in your other Booklets. To summarize them because they are beautiful, they are:

1. *Love your Father in Heaven above everything else.*
2. *Love your Neighbors as you love yourself.*
3. *Love your enemies also.*
    This is the formula for great love and contentment and beauty on earth for all of your Father's sacred children. There is no other way to achieve great peace across the whole world than this.

13. After a period of tribulation, the warning and miracle will occur in the same year. (Conchita, one of the four, as described the warning as a "correction of conscience" during which <u>everyone in the world will be given a revelation of the state of their souls before God.</u> We will see the consequences of our sins and will feel sorrow for them. The warning will be a moment of great grace for mankind. A true penetration of the Holy Spirit into our inmost Hearts, but it will be a traumatic event when we recognize the gravity of our sins and our distance from God.

Question: the correction of conscience has also been expressed as the illumination of conscience for every person on earth. Dear Mother, can you give more details on how this will happen and the relative timing of it perhaps?

Answer: *yes, this illumination of conscience will occur toward the last part of the tribulation worldwide. The earth will be already exhausted with all the people from the effects* *of their sinful behavior for all these hardships will have been in place for some years by then. It is then that your Heavenly Father will induce to everyone of His sacred children still on the earth making everyone's conscience very visible to them. And most importantly they will view their conscience in the same manner in which your Father views how they have sinned and importantly how all their sins have affected others of His sacred children. This will be the very last chance that all His sacred children will have to change their lives. And start to live their lives in accordance with the three rules that you my son have published and shown elsewhere in this magnificent Booklet you are writing for them.*

It is at this point; the wheat will be separated from the chaff, as my son said 2000 years ago. And it will become very visible to all who will choose eternal love as their destiny with their Father. Versus those who will reject their Father and will be banished to hell to be ultimately disintegrated back into nothingness as you have already written about my son. One other way of putting it, as you have also published my son, is we will be separating the sheep from the goats. Sheep to the right and goats to the left as my son has said while he was on the earth.

Our Blessed Mother spoke to them conveying messages vital not to just for Garabandal but for all of humanity. This message lamented the lack of dissemination of the first warning and highlighted that many religious leaders were leading souls to damnation and that the Eucharist was being neglected.

The Virgin Mary call for repentance prayer and sacrifice, reminding of Jesus's love and His passion before seen punishment will be a direct intervention from God making it extremely dreadful. It will be more painful for innocent children to endure this punishment than to die a natural death. Before the punishment Catholics should confess and others should repent. Even though Conchita saw the punishment alongside the Virgin Mary she felt immense fear. In his booklet, Francisco Sanchez Ventura Ipsquali quotes Conchita saying the punishment will depend on humanity's response to the divine messages and if it were to occur it would be extremely harsh.

Marie Cruz in a 2006 interview emphasized the Virgin was not threatening but rather warning as a loving Mother would. Conchita stated the Blessed Virgin Mary told her Jesus does not wish to send the punishment to distress us but to help and reprimand us.

Marie Lowly one of the four said Russia was suddenly and unexpectedly going to overrun a great part of the free world. Only a few years ago when this was written Russia invaded a large country in Europe called Ukraine.

The Pope and The End of Times

In 1963 Conchita, one of the visionaries of Garabandal conveyed a message from the Our Blessed Mother Mary that echoed the prophecy of Malachi. As many of you may know this prophecy pertains to the succession of Popes in the Catholic Church. <u>Our Blessed Mother Mary revealed to Conchita the prophecy of the three popes stating that after Pope John XXIII there would only be three more pontiffs before the End of Times. This is what was reported. However, people did not bother to report the very next sentence Blessed Mother Mary told Conchita which is actually there would be four popes not three. Because Mother Mary was not counting Pope John Paul I do to his very short reign.</u>

Conchita's exact words as recounted in a conversation with her mother. Her mother asked how she knew this; Conchita said the Virgin Mary told me. When asked if this meant the end of the world, Conchita clarified the Virgin Mary spoke of the End of Times, not the end of the world.

The prophecies from Blessed Mother Mary at Garabandal occurred during the pontificate of John Paul XXIII and Paul VI. After Pope John XXIII, we have had Paul VI, John Paul 1, John Paul II, Benedict XVI, and now Pope Francis. Excluding Pope John I, given the brevity of His pontificate, we arrive at Pope Francis as the third Pope after the prophecy of three more popes before the beginning of the End of Times.

Pope Francis — March 13, 2013-
Benedict XVI — April 19, 2005-Feb. 28, 2013.
John Paul II — Oct. 16, 1978-April 2, 2005.
John Paul I — Aug. 26-Sept. ... Too short to count.
Paul VI — June 21, 1963-Aug. 6, 1978.
John XXIII — Oct. 28, 1958-June 3, 1963.
Additional Evidence from St. Malachy In The 12th Century [11]

Saint Malachy was born in 1094 at Armagh, Ireland and died on November 2, 1148. St. Malachy was canonized in 1190 by Pope Clement III. This was the first papal canonization of an Irish saint. The source of the prophecy attributed to Him is still up for debate, but the following is how it is usually related:

While in Rome in 1139 St. Malachy received a vision showing Him all the Popes from His day to the end of time. He wrote poetic descriptions of each of the pontiffs and presented the complete manuscript to Pope Innocent II, but the prophecies were forgotten in the Vatican until 1590. These mottoes in the prophecies usually refer to a family name, birthplace, a coat-of-arms, or an office held before election to the papacy.

Now considering the papal succession. This has led many to ponder could Pope Francis be the Pope of the start of the End of Times as mentioned in the prophecy and what exactly does the end of times mean? [12]

The end of times should not be confused with the end of the world. It might signify a period of momentous change in the Church or the world's, a new era of evangelization or a profound spiritual reform. The congregation for the doctrine of the faith has never issued an official statement regarding the events of Garabandal, therefore the matter remains open both at the diocesan and Vatican levels.

---

[11] https://Catholicprophecy.org/st-malachy/

[12] https://Catholicprophecy.org/st-malachy/

Earth

She also brought warnings that are very fearful for the entire world. Mother Mary prophesized some information regarding the end of times. She said in the prophecy three popes remained and then the end of times would commence.

Most importantly what does our Blessed Mother say to us today in March 2024? As indicated before your author has been supremely Blessed and gifted by our loving Almighty Father in Heaven so I am able to hear the words of the Trinity and Our Blessed Mother Mary. The following are the words directly spoken to me from her, Our Blessed Mother Mary.

Question: Dear Mother Mary, all of the reporting regarding Garabandal has been from Conchita only one of the four children in the village. I am wondering why this is and why have the other three children not said anything or what they said was just not published?

Answer*: thank you for asking this last-minute question for it is a very good one. There are many reasons as I mentioned to you at another time that kept ever so many people that I talked to from reporting what I have said. You remember that I told you I appeared 375 times and only a handful of my apparitions were taken seriously and communicated to others of God sacred children.*

Mari Loli Mezon,
Jacinta González,
Mari Cruz González,
Maria "Conchita" Concepción.

All four of these girls were delightful and so receiving to my messages to them. in the case of the first girl on your list above she was very shy and was intimidated very easily. when Church officials came and started asking questions, she was very scared and did not want to say anything as a result. it was only much later in her life she started to talk about her experience with me.

With regards to Jacinta, she was much like Mari. Actually, all four of them were very shy. As time went on

Question: Dear Mother Mary, a number of people believe you indicated in your apparitions at Garabandal you said the Pope will travel to Moscow. Is that true or a stretch of imagination?

Answer: *Oh, my dear son, thank you for wanting to clear this up because so many of the things I said get twisted many ways. I indicated that the Pope would go to Russia, I did not ever say Moscow in particular. People tend to extend what I say beyond what I mean. This is the case in this instance. In addition to lamenting about the lack of distribution of my messages I also lament on the manner in which they are transmitted to others in a broken way. Thank you, dear son ever so much for providing me the opportunity to always as you would say, "set the record straight."*

Thank you, dear Mother Mary, and please always tell me everything you want me to pass on to God sacred children whatever it is you wish to say in the booklets I am writing. I love you.

Mother Mary: *I love you too my son.*

Prophecy Fulfilled? Pope Goes to Russia: Garabandal Interview with Glenn Hudson

As this is written April 3, 2024, there is talk in the media about Pope Francis visiting Moscow. Whether he goes not at this point in time is not certain. Time will tell because Russia right now is engaged in a terrible war with Ukraine. **Dr Taylor Marshall** [13]

Pope Wants to Go to Moscow to Meet Putin

Glenn Hudson and Taylor Marshall

The Pope has wanted to go since 2017.

Albrecht Weber **There was a message in 1965 about Russia.**

According to Glenn Hudson, recognized expert on Garabandal.

Before the warning, the miracle and the chastisement can happen. three events must happen before, there would be.

---

[13] Prophecy Fulfilled? Pope Goes to Russia: Garabandal Interview with Glenn Hudson (youtube.com) https://www.youtube.com/watch?v=plJVeWnOI_M

1. An important synod would take place, we have that right now.
2. Communism would return again; we can see this even within America now.
3. The Pope would go to Moscow, and as soon as he returns to the Vatican, hostilities will break out at different parts in Europe.

Mother Mary said this would not be World War III three separate times only when things get absolutely terrible would God then allow the warning which many people call the illumination of conscience so people would see themselves as God sees them.

The chronology:

1. The four popes ending with Pope Francis. The 112th pope.
2. Pope Francis going to Moscow.
3. Terrible hostilities will break out as soon as the pope returns to the Vatican in different parts of Europe. Things will get terribly worse than we ever imagined.
4. With Pope Francis we have now entered into the end of time or as Glenn Hudson puts it the beginning of a new era.
5. The great warning will be:
   a. there will be a suspension of time so that cars and planes will even stop when time stops. Note: Yes! God does have the power to stop time. Actually, we all do live within His eternal existence.
   b. Everyone on earth will see their sins of commission and omission not just Catholics. Everyone, please, remember we do not see our sins as God does and the gravity of the damage, they do to not only ourselves but others of God sacred children as well. People do not understand the impact their sins have on others of God's children. We do not understand the difference between lying and stealing for example, but we will find out during the illumination of conscience many times labeled as the warning.

c.   The chastisement which is most likely the three days of darkness that can be interpreted to be if people do not repent from their sins. Other possible punishments include, natural disasters resulting in awful suffering. All this is aimed to make mankind understand they will be doomed to hell if we do not change our Hearts and manner of conducting our lives.

6.   This is something Glenn Hudson surmised from all His research. There will be the greatest miracle ever performed at the pine trees were Blessed Mother Mary appeared to the four children at Garabandal. These pine trees, nine of them planted by Conchita grand Father which became Mother Mary's favorite place to appear. This will be permanent and a two-stage event. It will be about 15 minutes of something happening. And then it will become permanent left at Garabandal which will be our confirmation of what you felt during the warning which will then be obvious that it came from God.

In January 1966 Conchita visited the Vatican. Met with cardinals for several hours and the Pope. Paul. After a private interview, the Pope said, "I bless you and the whole Church blesses you too."

A final note about Garabandal

Blessed Mother Mary: *thank you my dear child for making all this effort in my behalf and the sacred children of your Heavenly Father. You are the only one that is able to and has taken the time and effort to spread my most vital messages to all His children on earth. As you know dear son, I have had horrible problems spreading my message to the world forever so many reasons. You have already experienced much of that with more to come. But take Heart son because in time everything you have written as you have said will ultimately become sacred messages to God's sacred children. What you have written does indeed amplify and extend our holy Bible and all the Biblical meanings contained within it.*

Regarding my messages at Garabandal you have covered them in this section of your booklet very well. There is nothing really more of substance that I can add to what you have already written. I have said many other things in my prophecies in other apparitions that I know you will include. So, I will wait for those and comment also on those when you get to them.

I love you, Blessed Mother Mary

Thank you, dear Mother Mary I will always do the absolute best, I can for you, I love you.

The Catholic Church is Very Concerned About These Mother Mary's Prophecies [14]

The Catholic Church is indeed worried about Mary's prophesies because she tells absolute pure and perfect truth. Much of what she says highlights the serious defects in the Vatican hierarchy. Plainly put, it goes beyond embarrassing and into breaches of credibility with a strong stench of Satanic activities. I will cover this point in another booklet that directly addresses the Vatican you thought you knew but just is NOT there anymore due to Pope Francis over the past decade.

Is the Pope Francis the Anti-Christ?

Dear brothers and sisters, we are not certain about the divine origin of the events at Garabandal. We await the Church's official stance. While many aspects suggest that something extraordinary might have occurred, only the Church can discern the truth of such phenomena.

At the end of the narrative by the Catholic Church regarding Garabandal, the authors get wishy-washy because they do not want to offend the current Church hierarchy. I sense fear in their conclusions using the words like "might have occurred," "something

---

[14] YouTube: https://www.youtube.com/watch?v=a_kiVfG5C8Q Why The Church is Terrified About These Children's Prophecy (youtube.com)

extraordinary," "many aspects" and so on. Let's face it, the Church hierarchy wants to avoid at all costs any reference to the 112th Pope being prophesies as not only the last Pope but an anti-Pope or the Anti-Christ. The political reasons are obvious.

Yet, from an ontological and visual perspective we see that for the female children personally witnessed divine powers upon them. And they honestly testified what they experienced and what they were told by two spiritual beings on many separate occasions. Additionally, there were many thousands of people that objectively observed the four girls in a state of ecstasy walking toward the pines Mother Mary appeared at.

That would be our Blessed Mother Mary and the Archangel Michael. Frankly, given the political atmosphere now reigning supreme in the highest levels of the Catholic Church, I doubt they will address any of this. Because it goes against their wishes and goals to integrate the Catholic Church into a Satanically guided one world government and one world religion.

Source: YouTube - Garabandal After the Visions – Garabandal Warnings

Commentary: Blessed Mother Mary

Zeitoun, Egypt [15]

Mother Speaks About Her Apparitions at Zeitoun

In this section, I want to give my thanks to Brian Kranick, footnoted below. For His excellent work in documenting our Blessed Mother Mary's apparitions at Zeitoun, Egypt along with the few others I will document below. I found their work was so good there was not a lot I could add other than my personal discussions with our Blessed Mother Mary. Discussions regarding adding additional light to why she chose to appear there and what were her goals in doing so.

---

[15] The Overlooked Marian Apparitions at Zeitoun, Egypt, Brian Kranick

Mother Mary Speaks to Me Personally

Mother Mary's thoughts as given to me in the month of April 2024 are indicated further down in this section of this Booklet as in all other parts as well. As a reminder your author has been enormously Blessed by our Heavenly Father to have the ability to speak with the members of the holy Trinity and our Blessed Mother Mary. Like others of God sacred children, our Blessed Mother Mary speaks with me personally and answers my questions about her apparitions and various times in different places. I am not the only one in addition to a few others during her apparitions.

Remember, please, Our Blessed Mother Mary also spoke to many people over the last hundred years to bring her message of love, penance, sacrifice, encouraging praying the rosary and receiving the sacraments on a regularly. Additionally, Mother Mary has stated that if enough people do what I just mentioned many wars would have been avoided.

This Heavenly gift to me Jesus Christ told me was because of a conversation I had with our Almighty Father before I was born to the earth. This is true by the way, for all of you. All of us were created in the blink of an eye by our Heavenly Father in the Heavenly Kingdom unknown billions of years ago. Each of us is one-of-a-kind, unique from everyone else yet we have great commonality as well. Our Heavenly Father loved each of us so much he left a part of Himself within our spiritual being. So, when we came to earth for the "earth test" he would be with us every instant of our lives. In this way our Father could experience every detail of our lifetime and it would be impossible for Him to not hear every prayer we have ever said. When people say God is closer than we think, they are precisely correct. You can find more detail of this particular thought in the previously published Booklet titled, "God's Grand Design, Booklet I, Creation."

This apparition of Our Blessed Mother Mary is unique as she never said one word to anybody during the many hundreds of times, she appeared above the Coptic Church in the Zeitoun district of Cairo.

A Short History of Zeitoun

In the 1920s a Coptic Christian named Tawfik Khalil Abraham owned some land and wanted to build a hotel there. But Mother Mary had other ideas. She appeared to Tawfik in a dream and asked him to build a Coptic Church instead that would be in her honor. Whether he knew or not that the site of his hotel was where the holy family stayed escaping the slaughter from King Herod in Jerusalem. If he built the Church, Mother Mary promised a miracle there sometime in the future. Thus, her apparitions starting in 1968.

Question: dear Mother Mary I think we know why you chose Zeitoun for three years of your holy apparitions. It is because this is where you and the rest of the holy family came to escape Herod's killing of innocent children. Is this true? And what else would you like others of God sacred children to know.

Answer*: Yes, my dear son we in the holy family were there but not for all of the time before we went back to Jerusalem. We chose Zeitoun also because it is what you would say a melting pot of many different religious beliefs. Of course, Islam and Christianity are the top two. I wanted to demonstrate a message that the holy Trinity in me is for everyone no matter their beliefs. However, you have already written about the chances of different religions have in order to enter the Heavenly Kingdom. As my son told you, only 6% of Muslims make it into the Heavenly Kingdom. The ones that make it our those who remain silent in their Godly Christian beliefs. In an atmosphere of violence toward those who do not accept the impostor God called Allah this is the only way they can survive and be welcomed into your Father's holy kingdom.*

I wanted to project God's beautiful love to everybody and not just a few this time that I appeared. As you already described in this booklet, I was able to simultaneously look into the eyes of all the people and give them my blessings. And especially show them that there is far more to their existence than just the physical aspects. My appearance shows that even though I said nothing they knew I was real. Because I made it a point to move around on the top of the

Coptic Church and raise my hands blessing them. They also knew I was real because the wind would move my garments around to prove I was alive and with them. I wanted very much to show all the people no matter their station in life that ultimately, they are all sacred children of their Father.

I wanted to demonstrate that the divisions that separate the people into different groups are not of God, they are only of human imagination. So many killings, deaths, and wars are the result of human Satanic imaginations. All of God's sacred children are completely equal in the eyes of their Father. Yes, they are unique as you have said many times my son. But these differences allow each of God's sacred children to express their individuality but that is based solely on their loving identity as sacred children of your Father. This is also part of the reason I did not want to say anything but just let people gaze upon me then realize they are all one Blessed family.

I was very happy to see that one man saw my teeth when I smiled. This was a great detail of my appearance that you included in this Booklet. Yes, my dear son, I do have teeth! This is very funny to me. It is too bad that the people did not have color photography because I did appear in color the way in which you always see me standing next to you dear son.

Mother Mary's Apparitions in Zeitoun Cairo Egypt

These apparitions of our Blessed Mother Mary are very unique. Not only were her apparitions witnessed by millions, but she never said one word to anybody during the many hundreds of times she appeared above the Coptic Christian Church in the Zeitoun district of Cairo.

Zeitoun – The Many Apparitions

These apparitions of Our Blessed Mother are unique; not only did she remain silent during them, but conditions were such, pictures could be taken of her. Some movies were taken as well that actually showed her garments rustling in the wind. This is the technology that existed in the early 1960s. Later with advanced photography techniques, which allowed manipulation of the images to reveal the facial image of our Blessed Mother as shown below. It has been enhanced to bring out the details that were not able to be seen before.

This picture has been photo enhanced with new computer technology so is to bring out details of our Blessed Mother Mary that were not available before. I find this picture to be completely fascinating considering I have spoken with Mother Mary directly on many occasions. It is only now I can see her in a great amount of detail. When she first approached me with our Lord and Savior Jesus Christ a number of years ago, I did see her in full living color along with Jesus. However as is the case within the spiritual realm, knowing a person's identity does leave out in almost all cases their spiritual facial features. Please consider this to be a magnificent revelation of our Blessed Mother Mary.

Key Facts About Blessed Mother Mary's Apparitions

Her apparitions started in April 1968 and ended in May 1971. She would appear three or four times per month above St. Mary's Coptic Church in Zeitoun where everyone could see her. Unlike Garabandal Spain, everyone could see her as she appeared on the rooftop. She would move around and at times smile and wave to the crowds giving them her blessings. One witness got close enough to where he said he could see her teeth when she smiled.

In total, it is estimated that hundreds of thousands to millions of people saw her in person. The people included Coptics, Catholics, Protestants, and even some secular Marxists. Egyptian President Abdel Nasser a Muslim also witnessed her apparition. It is thought the reason Mary appeared was because history shows the holy family stayed there for a time to avoid Herod's slaughter of the innocents. This occurred when he found out the child of God had been born in Jerusalem. The holy family fled to Egypt and Zeitoun is one of the places they stayed.

What did Mother Mary's apparitions look like?

Mother Mary's apparitions typically began as a ball of light then Eve all loving into taking on her form as our Blessed Mary. It wasn't just her image of light that occurred but also at times large numbers of luminous doves flew across the sky sometimes in the formation of a cross. It is also reported that many healings happened as well. These healings included blindness, cripples, polio, cancer, and other terminal illnesses.

Mary was dressed in white and blue robes and a veil of bluish white light. Her halo was also of right light. Some of the witnesses indicated they also saw her with the infant Jesus or sometimes Jesus as 12 years old and other times with St. Joseph as well. Additionally, she was at times seen carrying a cross or in olive branch which is a plea for peace and unity. A Coptic priest is credited with saying that beautiful rays of light came down from her hands like depicted in the miraculous metal.

One extremely interesting observation reported by Coptic Bishop Marcos said that when Mother Mary looked at the crowd, it was as if she was simultaneously concentrating her eyes on each person in the crowd separately. It was as if she was concentrating on each person and looking at each person separately and individually. Needless to say, her apparitions also resulted in spiritual conversions of Muslims and others to Christianity.

The Vatican response about Zeitoun:

The Vatican even after three years of Marian apparitions refused to make an official statement regarding Zeitoun. I have no idea why the Vatican would turn its back on this and instead said the deferred this whole episode to the Coptic Orthodox Church. Appropriately, the Coptic Church did investigate the matter and determined it was an authentic and true phenomenon. Not only that, but the civil government also concluded that something very real was happening. The local civil authorities went so far in their investigation they cut off all electric power in a radius of 15 miles from the Coptic Church where Mother Mary was appearing. This was to eliminate the possibility that somehow a projector was being used to create her image. They found that no projectors could possibly be used and when they shut off the power our Blessed Mother Mary, her image remained as bright as ever.

The Catholic Church in my view has a very irritating tendency of turning their back on legitimate holy spiritual phenomenon. In the case of Garabandal for example in spite of all the wonderful evidence of Mother Mary's apparitions, the Catholic Church in the Vatican refused to acknowledge it. It is your author's opinion that the reason for this is part of the prophecies from Mother Mary involve the 112th Pope being the last pope and very likely the Anti-Christ. The Vatican magisterium who is more and more promoting Satanically inspired political judgments in the form of pronouncements for all Catholics are afraid whatever Blessed Mother Mary said in her apparitions makes them look bad. Well, they are! Not all of them but enough.

If we examine Pope Francis and what he has been doing, it's fair to say he is secularizing our beloved Catholic Church into blessing all sorts of condemned behavior as taught by Biblical scripture. A detailed discussion of this can be found in another section of this booklet.

5

Mother Mary Describes Fatima 1, Fatima 2, and Fatima 3

Author's Note: I have purposely left the apparitions of Blessed Mother Mary till after all the painful wretched information about the sad conditions of our beloved Catholic Church these days. By doing this you can see how the dishonesty of the Vatican plays out with regard to Blessed Mother Mary's apparitions at Fatima. The Vatican felt it was forced to lie terribly about going so far as to make Lucia disappear to a convent that hid her from telling the truth about what Mother Mary told her. An imposter Sister Lucia was made into a public figure telling the world the Vatican lies about Fatima.

Little does our criminal Vatican know you are reading the book that documents the exact truth about Fatima because that comes directly from Blessed Mother Mary herself.

A Fundamental Description of All Three Fátima Revelations

Fátima is one of the most well-known apparitions of our Blessed Mother Mary. Like many others of her apparitions, she chose three little children to speak to. In our Lady's multiple apparitions from May 13, 1917, until October 1917, she revealed apocalyptic visions and prophecies. These prophecies were told to three young Portuguese shepherds, Lúcia Santos, Jacinta, and Francisco Marto.

One may ask why is it Our Blessed Mother Mary chooses young children to tell her prophecies. Our Blessed Mother personally told me [16] that it is because young children have not been on the earth long

---

[16] Just as our Blessed Mother Mary speaks to God's sacred children across the world so too does she speak to me as I write Christian spiritual literature. I am our Heavenly Father 's "Anointed Messenger" (continued)

enough to have their consciousness or worldview tainted by Satanic influences. Yes, dear reader, as I said before, I've been chosen and gifted by Our Heavenly Father to speak with Him, our Lord and Savior Jesus Christ, the Holy Spirit, and our Blessed Mother Mary. Both our Lord Jesus and our Blessed Mother Mary have had occasions in the past to speak with certain sacred children of God while they are on the earth.

Each of the children that have been chosen by the Divine Will have been chosen very carefully for specific reasons. It is actually a wonderful thing to live your life knowing how close you are to the Trinity and our Blessed Mother Mary. It does bring with it certain amounts of trials and tribulations. It can be exceedingly difficult too. But the loving rewards and the magnificent feelings of the love from being so close to our Heavenly Father, Lord Jesus Christ the Holy Spirit and our Blessed Mother far outweigh any of the sufferings. I would not have it any other way.

It is important to note Our Blessed Mother Mary did not just pop out of nowhere and start talking to these children. That would have scared the living daylights out of them, and they would probably and rightly run for the hills. What happened instead was the apparition of Blessed Mother Mary actually started in 1916, the previous year. The children's guardian angel coming to them and teaching them prayers and reparations to the Blessed Sacrament and then giving them the holy Eucharist.

Now back to Fátima. As always, our Blessed Mother speaks of love, penance, sacrifice, prayer and receiving the holy sacraments very often. She encourages prayer at least twice a day with the Our Father and the Hail Mary. This is essential to a healthy Christian life. But regarding Fátima in 1917 her message was much different. She

---

(continued) and have written a sacred book with our Heavenly Father, our Lord and Savior Jesus Christ, our Holy Spirit, and our Blessed Mother Mary. The other masterpiece book is titled "God's Grand Design of All Creation for Your Redemption." It reveals our Heavenly Father's message to all His sacred children on earth and reveals advanced theology that extends our Biblical literature.

carried with her divine messages and warnings and signs of prophecies God's sacred children must be aware of. I know it hurt Blessed Mother to deliver these messages. But it is completely necessary because it is a very loving thing to do to warn people of terrible things coming their way unless they changed the path they are on.

Question: Dearest Mother Mary, knowing you as I do, I can only imagine the pain you must have felt when you delivered the messages and their contents to the three shepherds in Fátima. If you do not want to answer this, I fully understand. But what was it like for you, what were your feelings when you were delivering the warnings and other messages to the three girls?

Answer*: I thank you, my dear son, for being sensitive to my feelings. I know you have loved me so much all these years and you are not afraid to show your love for me and your concern for my feelings. Earlier when you asked me about the Gospel of Thomas[17] you were afraid that it would cause me too much pain. I thank you for that. But I gave you a short answer and I know you felt bad asking the question, but it needed to be told how terrible and fraudulent that gospel really was and the reasons why.*

Regarding Fátima, I felt like this was just something necessary to do. Because, for me I was doing everything I could for humankind, your Father's sacred children, so they would avoid the awful chastisements that were coming quite quickly in human history. Yes, dear son, I felt awful yet like any mother on earth knows, you must always do anything you can to protect your children from making terrible mistakes. This is what I did. But much of my warnings were not heeded in a painful history, which developed in the coming years. I always lament about how God's sacred children tend to not pay attention and go about their business no matter how self-destructive it is, they just keep doing what they always have. I know you have experienced this, my son, with your first book, God's

---

Booklet #2: Blessed Mother Mary Reveals Her Apparitions

Grand Design of all Creation for your Redemption. That book should be on the worldwide best seller list, but people are too caught up in the attractive Satanic temptations that taste good and feel good without any concern for their eternal destiny. I love you, my dear son.

Question: dear Mother Mary: from what I observe, you are very unhappy as you just revealed regarding the reception of Fátima throughout the world. I can only assume that this is why you felt it necessary to appear again at Akita Japan with Sister Sasagawa[18]. Is this correct?

Answer: *Yes, my son, you are so perceptive as always. My warnings got tangled up in the politics of the Catholic Church and the Vatican. They were damaging God's sacred children by keeping things so secret that even when I wanted the third secret to be released fully throughout the world in 1960. The Vatican put up roadblocks to do that. And as you have said dear son, they did this for only internal political reasons. They are guilty of damaging your holy Father's sacred children across the entire world by hiding key information that I told the girls from being distributed around the world. Instead of serving God's sacred children, the cardinals and the bishops in the Vatican were more concerned about how they looked politically in their own minds. These are grave sins, and they will be punished accordingly. I hate to say that dear son, because it is painful but what else is there to say but that.*

I love the fact, dear son, that you never shy away from telling the truth of things. Thank you for knowing full well that my son is the way the truth and the life, and no one comes to the Father except through Him. There will come a day, dear son, when there will be occasions that many people want to hear your words of love and advanced theology from the message of your Father. But not quite yet.

---

[18] Our Lady's apparition, Akita, Japan

On that particular note dear Blessed Mother Mary, I look forward to the day when there are many people with open hearts to hear the message of our loving Almighty Father. For the first time they will understand His message of peace, love, understanding, acceptance along with advanced theology that makes it possible to understand how all creation works together in such a beautiful way.

Back in 1917 when Our Blessed Mother appeared on six separate occasions to three little shepherds in Portugal, there were three secrets of Fátima that were revealed to these three Portuguese children. The "secrets" were actually prophecies and are only called secrets because the Catholic Church wanted to control these prophecies and keep them secret from God's sacred children. The secrets of Fátima occurred toward the end of World War I which happened from July 28, 1914, to November 11, 1918.

The fundamental content of Fátima was warnings things would get a lot worse in the future unless God's sacred children turn away from Satanic behavior. The first two Fátima secrets were revealed in 1941 in a document written by Lucia at the request of José Alves Correia da Silva, Bishop of Leiria. It was not until 1943 when the secrets of Fátima were completely revealed. In October 1943, the Bishop of Leiria ordered Lucia to put the secrets in writing. Lucia wrote down the third secret and sealed it in an envelope not to be opened until 1960.

It is especially important to note the three children were obeying what Blessed Mother Mary told them to do. In this case the third secret, it was not to be revealed until the year of 1960. However, due to unknown actions within the Vatican, the third secret was not revealed as Blessed Mother Mary requested. It was not until Pope John Paul II officially released the third secret, or what the Vatican called the Third Secret. This caused tremendous speculation the Pope withheld vital information about the third secret.

However, even then, only part of the third secret was revealed by the Pope. The Vatican withheld all the information about coming tribulations and that the 112th Pope would be the last and be highly likely also be the anti-Christ. The Vatican wanted this part of the third secret to remain secret and hidden in the Vatican. There was even more within the third secret that was also not revealed defying the requests of Our Blessed Mother Mary. To this day, their disobedience angers me greatly.

Fatima Apparition 1 [19]

This first secret was a very disturbing vision of hell. To a young girl this must have been an awful experience to realize such things do exist. Lucia has indicated in her third memoir published in 1941 that this first so-called secret was told to her and the other two children on July 13, 1917.

She went on to say, "Our Lady showed us a great sea of fire which seemed to be under the earth. Plunged into this fire were demons and souls in human form. Like transparent burning embers. All blackened or burnished bronze. Floating about in the conflagration. Now raised into the air by the flames that ensued from within themselves. To gather with great clouds of smoke. Now falling back on every side like sparks in a huge fire, without weight or equilibrium, and amid shrieks and groans of pain and despair, which horrified us and made us tremble with fear."

As Our Heavenly Father's anointed messenger compared. The description of hell is given to the three children with what our Lord and Savior Jesus Christ told me. Yes, there is great suffering, but the suffering is not necessarily fire and brimstone. Rather <u>the suffering each person experiences is the horrific regret that comes from how they lived their lives while on earth</u>.

Before entering hell, each of God's sacred children does indeed meet personally with Jesus Christ. Every detail of their lives is there to witness in an atmosphere of pure and perfect love. It's during this review, which is referred to as "judgment" each sacred child sees everything they ever did, every thought, every motivation, and what they failed to do. Importantly they also saw the effects their sinful behavior had on others of God's sacred children. You cannot

---

[19] Wikipedia, three secrets of Fátima.

overestimate the importance of seeing the effect each of the condemned people their actions had in destroying others of God's sacred children.

Again, this is done in a pure and perfect loving atmosphere with some angels also present. Fundamentally it will become very apparent that for sinful people, there is no way they can be admitted to the Heavenly Kingdom. This is when yelling and screaming and gnashing of teeth occurs when they realize they will go to hell. It is then and while in hell their enormous regrets haunt them every moment of their existence from that point on.

One thing that is never discussed but is included in the sacred book I wrote with Jesus that says hell is actually not for all eternity. Rather because of the law of disintegration as Jesus says or the law of entropy as our scientists say, all things in hell decay back into the nothingness from whence they were created. Everyone in hell will ultimately dissolve back into nothingness which includes even the memories of people that knew them. There will be NO memories of people who went to hell. In other words, hell has been designed to slowly disintegrate back into the nothingness from which it originally came from. Yes, the sacred children of Almighty God are eternal and NOT subject to the law of denigration or entropy as scientists refer to it.

For those who are scientifically oriented the definition of entropy is the measure of randomness or chaos within a closed is the measure of randomness or chaos within a closed system. If you wonder why, you are getting wrinkles and losing hair as you age, that is a beautiful demonstration of entropy working on your body.

And so, it will be for those citizens of hell except entropy will not stop until the very last molecules of their existence dissolve back into the nothingness that originally existed. This is a magnificent plan by Our Heavenly Father because the end point of this will simply be a heavenly realm occupied by all spiritual entities that love our Almighty Father with all their heart. The rest of those that chose to rebel against our Father will be long gone to the point where no one will even remember them.

Question: Dear Blessed Mother Mary, somehow, I think I am losing some information regarding the first apparition at Fátima. I would appreciate any of your comments in to address anything I missed.

Answer*: Thank you for asking me this especially important question. What I told the children was exactly correct however their fear got in the way of a few things. When a person is in hell one size does not fit all so to speak. Their punishments and just Tizen mints are closely related to what they did to others of God's sacred children while they we are on earth. In other words, hell is tailor-made for each individual person. If someone, for example, cheated another person out of a considerable sum of money. The cheater being in heaven will experience a horrifically intensified feeling of severe loss that their victim felt while their victim was on earth.*

Likewise, if the person in hell was violent, they would experience the pain that they caused the other sacred child of God to feel. Except in hell the pain is intensified. They will also feel the agony of those closely related to the victim of their violence. They would feel their remorse, they would feel the concern and the feeling of complete helplessness as it related to the victim. Everything they caused other people will come back at them in an amplified manner.

As you know, my dear son, each and every citizen of hell was exposed to the pure and perfect love of heaven. That memory of pure love and now the complete loss of it knowing that they can never have it is something that will torment them for the rest of their existence. Until as you say dear son entropy catches up with them and dissolves them back into the nothingness from whence, they came.

So, when people talk about seeing the fires and brimstone of hell, in a way, that is correct. Because the citizens of hell have their souls on fire, the fire of experiencing all the torment that they caused others of God's sacred children on earth. There used to be a saying in the country you live in, "<u>What goes around comes around</u>."

My dearest son, the opposite is also true for people that are allowed through the singular gate to the Heavenly Kingdom. Throughout the life on earth of people in heaven they get to experience all the love, kindness, and beauty that they gave to others of God's sacred children. The more you have loved on earth the more you will experience love in heaven. And, of course, this is in addition. To the enormous beauty and emotional impact of your Heavenly Father's love. For each and every one of his sacred children who chose him and lived by his rules on earth, which is no easy task to do.

Dear Blessed Mother, this makes so much sense because there is a feedback mechanism in operation even on earth regarding the way people live their lives on this planet. If you treat people badly you will be treated badly, if you love them, you will get love in return. The way you described hell makes complete sense to me. Thank you, a million times, over for sharing this with our Father's sacred children.

You are so very welcome my dear son.

Fátima Apparition 2 [20]

From Lucia's Writings What Mother Mary Said to Her

"To save the poor sinners in hell God wishes to establish in the world a devotion to my Immaculate Heart. If what I say to you is done, many souls will be saved and there will be peace."

"The war is going to end (WWI) but if people do not cease offending God, a worse one will break out during the Pontificate of Pope Pius XI.

"When you see a night illumined by an unknown light, know that this is the great sign. Given you by God that he is about to punish the world for its crimes, by means of war, famine, and persecutions of the Church and of the Holy Father. If my requests are heeded, Russia will be converted, and there will be peace; if not, she will spread her errors throughout the world, causing wars and persecutions of the Church. The goodwill be martyred; the Holy Father will have much to suffer; various nations will be annihilated. In the end, my Immaculate Heart will triumph. The Holy Father will

---

[20] Wikipedia, Martins, Dr. António María, Memórias e cartas de Irmã Lúcia (Porto, Portugal: Simão Guimarães,   Filhos, LDA, 1973), 225.

consecrate Russia to me, and she shall be converted, and a period of peace will be granted to the world. " [21]

Fatima's Secret Apparition 3

My dear Blessed Mother Mary, I sincerely apologize for all the time it has taken me to come to this moment where you and I can talk about the famous third secret of Fatima. As you know dear Mother, I have done a lot of reading in preparation for speaking with you. This is because I do not want to insult you by being unprepared but rather being able to ask intelligent questions.

These so-called sources of the third secret of Fatima simply nibble around the edges of the subject matter without revealing the substance of what the third secret you told Lucia, Jacinta and Franciso. Many people say they have seen the third secret and have read it. But nobody has the guts to actually write down what they saw and reveal it to God's sacred children after 1960 which is per your request. All of them hide behind things saying they have taken an oath or been bound to keep things secret. I find that reprehensible and keeping secrets is hardly ever a good thing.

Dear reader, before we directly address what the third secret of Fatima says I must, I have to present to you some terrible ugliness that has arisen out of the Catholic Church years ago. Sister Lucia was a teller of truth. She was extremely upset regarding the contents of the third secret. But in the end because of heavenly intervention, she relented and wrote down what Blessed Mother Mary told her. Later in the text below you will read exactly what Blessed Mother Mary told me. Mother Mary also said Sister Lucia got almost everything correct regarding her description of what Mother Mary told her many years earlier.

Note: What you are going to read are the exact words Blessed Mother Mary has told me about Fatima.

---

[21] Santos, Fatima in Lucia's Own Words I (2003), pgs. 123–124.

Also, to remind you that as Blessed Mother Mary speaks to me, I use speech to text software to instantly transcribe every word Blessed Mother Mary says. Nobody, and I mean absolutely nobody has tampered with the words in this book. It is the real thing!

Now, please read the ugliness that came from the Catholic Church many years ago. If you sense I am angry about this situation you are absolutely right. I am damned enraged by what was done regarding the third secret and Lucia.

What is a reliable Catholic Christian Catechism.

It used to be Catholics could rely on the authenticity of the Catholic Catechism. No longer. Ever since Cardinal Bergoglio became pope, our catechism has been infiltrated over time into a blend of "Woke" political viewpoints. The goal of this pope is to blend Christian Catholicism with all the other religions in the world so as to "meet the needs of the people." In other words, throw out our beloved Bible and create a bastardized version of both the Bible and our Catechism that includes elements of progressive liberal political morality, Islam, Buddhism and so on.

I have already talked about how the "woke" Church has embedded itself within it is organizations then to mount attacks against true Christianity. This has been increasing by the Catholic Church attacking within itself as it can be observed manifesting itself over the last decade. So, what is a loving Catholic Christian sacred child of Almighty God to do? I for one cannot say definitively. I do have a master's degree in Pastoral ministry and theology which leads me to cry at the inner turmoil the Church is experiencing. I no longer take what the Vatican says as true. It just is not. I must be very skeptical and take the Vatican with an exceptionally large grain of salt and suspicion of the hidden agenda I am documenting within this book.

My answer to a loving sacred child of God is to <u>get hold of a Catholic catechism that was printed more than 10 years ago</u>. Why 10 years? It is because that is how long cardinal Bergoglio aka, Pope Francis has been the pope. Back then, he did not have time to poison the catechism yet. Same thing for our beloved Bible. I have always liked the King James Version. I have located what I believe is a reliable Catholic Catechism. It can be purchased on Amazon. Its publication date is 1995. [22]

Question: My dearest loving Blessed Mother Mary, is this the best advice I can give to all of God's sacred children, so they avoid treacherous woke-twisted theology from the Vatican these days? If I am wrong about this please dear Mother Mary tell me and your words will remain in this book dedicated to you

Answer: *Oh, my dear son, my dear child I continue to be amazed at the depth of your perceptions regarding their wretchedness of what is happening within our beloved Catholic Church. My dear son, you are 100% correct and you are correct for the very reasons that you have mentioned. I do worry however about the ability of your Father 's sacred children to obtain a Catholic catechism that was printed that far ago. Perhaps that is something each of your Father 's sacred children can look up for themselves. But yes, dear son, you have given loving Catholic Christians the absolute right advice so as to not be misled by Satan himself through the evil workings of the Vatican.*

Thank you, so very much dear son,
your Blessed Mother Mary

Thank you, dear Blessed Mother Mary. I am so glad I gave good information.

6

The Real 3rd Secret of Fatima from Blessed Mother Mary

A Magnificent Dialog

Now! Please compare the Pope's falsehoods about the third secret of Fatima with what our Beloved Blessed Mother actually said here! Please remember she spoke the following words directly to me, our Almighty Father 's Anointed Messenger. I have no affiliation with the Vatican and so I cannot be pressured in any way.

In order for Satan to accomplish his evil agenda, he must have the world believing the falsehood that the third secret of Fatima has been fulfilled. This is why the Pope said that. Again, the truth is that the third secret has NOT been fulfilled and Russia has NOT been consecrated to the Immaculate Heart of Blessed Mother Mary!

April 11, 2024

The Third Secret of Fatima directly Spoken by Our Blessed Mother Mary to Our Heavenly Father's Anointed Messenger: Richard Ferguson

So Here It Begins.

There will be wars and rumors of wars throughout the land. Millions upon millions of people good and bad will perish at the hands of others of God's sacred children. The entire earth will tremble and suffer for what has been caused by the evil one and His followers among God's sacred children on earth.

The Sky Will Blacken Like It Has Never Done Before.

If you reach out your hand you will not be able to see it. The light from candles will not be seen. This will frighten every one of God

sacred children on the earth. But this will happen in the very near future, my dearest son.

Things will start to get slowly gray and then grayer and grayer still until the gray will come completely black. This will be like no black mankind has ever seen before. Your Father's sacred children have always enjoyed the illumination of the sun. But during this time there will be no light at all. <u>Nothing will be seen not even the fingers at the end of people's hands</u> can be seen. There will be some time before everything is completely black. During this period of increasing grayness toward black your loving Father is giving His sacred children a chance. To come together with their loved ones before everything becomes the blackest of black beyond which there is nothing blacker.

Question: Dear Blessed Mother, I am almost 80 years old. Will I experience this with my family?

Answer: *Yes, my dear son. This will happen toward the end of your earthly existence so please warn your family of what is to come. I know that your son will not believe you, as he has not believed all the things you have taught him in his life. And as a result, he has made many mistakes that he will pay for now and will continue such.*

Of the time until everything is completely black. The time for the start of the grayness to the blackness will give those of God's children time enough to come together with their loved ones. This is an act of love from your Almighty Father in Heaven.

Because of the blackness people will not be able to find food or water to sustain themselves. This is also on purpose my dear son because it is not food that sustains God sacred children but the magnificent overwhelming love of your Father.

People Will Pray Like They Have Never Prayed Before.

For it is always the case that it takes great fear to bring people to God. This is such a shameful thing, yet it is true. My dear son, there are very few people like you that have such an intense love for your Heavenly Father. Such that you have never been scared of Him but rather you have had a deep-seated love for Him before you came to earth.

The blackening of the earth is the warning to pray. After three days, which is really a little longer than three days, slowly the blackness will begin to dissipate. And after a time, people will start to be able to see very short distance and be able to see the fingers on the end of their arms.

It is good that you digest this first before I continue onward.

My dear son, would you like me to now talk about the Church?

Our Beloved Church

Yes, Mother Mary because part of the third secret is already starting to happen.

Again, my dear son, your perception is wonderful. I know that over the last six months, as you have been observing the Vatican and the current Pope, you have been getting more and more agitated. Realizing that this Pope wants to subjugate my son's Holy Church to the wretched political powers that exist on this earth.

My son, although, He (Our Beloved Father) is ever so forgiving is also very upset about this. Yet, the Trinity and I know these things must happen to fulfill the prophecies that have been made over the last thousands of years and are indeed in our Holy Bible. Which includes not only the New Testament but portions of the Old Testament as well.

<u>*Your current Pope has said the anti-pope is now on the earth. He should know because… He Is That Anti-Pope.*</u>

What is unknown to the innocent sacred children of God is that behind the scenes this Pope has been arranging for not only a one-world government under Satan but also a one-world Church under Satan. That is completely against the teachings of my beloved Son. The end goal of the Satanic plan is to subjugate your Father's sacred children into a system that brings together their falsehoods in Almighty God. As well as domination of every particle of their existence while they were on earth by Satanic forces that will stop at nothing to rule over every aspect of their physical existence.

Your Father will allow all of this to happen so that once and for all people will see that the source of all love, the source of all goodness is your Heavenly Father. When He withdraws His love from the people on earth things will become unbearable in a very short period of time.

Satan Will Place Himself on The Throne of Peter in The Vatican

Yes, my dear son, and as you would say my son all hell will break out. There is not one thing that a sacred child of God can do that must first be approved by Satan's demons visible now on earth.

Satan's Earthly Power:

The Vatican will then become the center of all earthly power headed up by Satan Himself. He will rule with an iron fist through a cadre in layers of authority much like any military would have today. There will be small amounts of commerce that occur across the earth but there will be no tattoos of the number 666 as so many people believe. As you know my dear son, there are no secrets in the spiritual realm. Everyone's identity will automatically be known by Satan Himself and all of His demons.

Without labels, Satan's government will know who everyone is and whether or not they are willing to follow Him so as to survive just for a tiny bit more time on an increasingly painful earth. You and your family, my son, however, because of your intense love for your Father, the Trinity and me, will not have to suffer this. You and they will be taken up as well as many into the Heavenly Kingdom in the blink of an eye.

There will be mass executions of God's sacred children who refuse Satan and bodies will pile higher and higher and higher and the stench of their rotten corpses will fill the air for miles around. Many will be tortured just as the Romans did during the times of my son. Satan's demons will enjoy doing this to God's sacred children. They know that their time is getting very short.

All of the so-called laws of the earth will emanate from St. Peter's throne in the Vatican. All this will be allowed to happen by the Catholic Church as it descends deeper into Satanic treachery and debauchery of a magnitude that, my dear son, will make you completely sick to your stomach. My dear son, as you have already uncovered in your research you have seen pictures of the current pope being entertained by scantily clad women. Dancing in front of him with many of his sick Cardinals sitting behind him. So, show this to the world, my dearest son, show all of it.

Also, my dear son there will be earthquakes such that the world has never seen before. No continent will be spared not even Antarctica, which people in the northern hemisphere never think about. None will be spared, both the good and the evil.

I know my dear son that there will be suffering but only for instant before they (my family and I) are in the arms of your Lord and Savior Jesus and our Holy Almighty Father. This will be true for you and your family. However, in the case of your son, he will be asked if he wants to go to Heaven or lead his life like he always has that leads to hell. He will be afforded this question only because he is in your family. Otherwise, he is considered a nonbeliever and will suffer with all the other nonbelievers.

The others that do not believe their suffering will be far longer and stretched out before they are condemned into the realm of hell never to be heard from again. And, my dear son, as you have written in your first book God's Grand Design and the Booklet 1 Creation that is soon to be published, they will be doomed. To dissolving back into nothing from whence they came.

These earthquakes, both on the continents and under the sea, will be so great that tsunamis will be so great that they will wash up on the land as much as 100 miles inland. And wash away all life that was once there. There will be no escape for anyone from any of this. Yet this is not all.

The Long-Awaited Consecration of Russia to The Immaculate Heart of Blessed Mother Mary

In your mind now I can see that the topic of world wars has come. Yes, my son, your worst fears will come true. There was a time not too long ago when World War III could have been avoided and the timetable for this in times would have been pushed back. That timetable was when I asked the Pope to consecrate Russia into my Immaculate Heart. This caused great division among the bishops and cardinals in the Church at the time. How foolish and shortsighted can they be?

In 1962, only two years after I asked the third secret to be released to God's sacred children, the Pope wanted to consecrate Russia to my sacred Heart. However great pressure was put upon him by the magisterium not to do that for shortsighted reasons. All Pope John Paul had to say in His opening prayer was:

<u>*"And now I consecrate all of Russia to the Immaculate Heart of our Blessed Mother Mary."*</u>

Author's note: It should be restated that there have been multiple popes that refused to consecrate Russia in the past in addition to wanting to keep the third secret of Fatima secret as well.

The people of Russia would be overjoyed, and things would start to go into a loving direction. Instead, the Pope referred to Russia in an indirect and oblique manner which frankly did nothing at all.

As I tell you this my dear son, I know that your Pope Francis talks about doing this but as you like to say at times, "don't hold your breath." <u>The last thing this Anti-Christ wants to do is to bring peace in the world.</u>

Question: Dear Mother Mary, on this point, one of our news outlets said Pope Francis consecrated Russia? did Pope Francis consecrate Russia?

Answer: *My dear son, NO<u>!</u> Pope Francis did not. He said a few prayers about Russia, but he did not invoke the consecration to my Immaculate Heart. His goal was to fool a lot of people which he succeeded in doing.*

Question: Did Pope Francis ever go to Russia?

Answer: *No, he did not, and as your research shows he met with Putin at the Russian embassy. There were a lot of prayers that were* said, and they gave the impression that Pope Francis consecrated Russia.

Pope Francis purposely did not say the words necessary to consecrate Russia to my Immaculate Heart. Pope Francis did not say: "And Now I Consecrate All of Russia To The Immaculate Heart Of Our Blessed Mother Mary."

He purposely fooled the entire world. My dear son, you never liked Francis from the very beginning. You even did not like him before he was inaugurated as Pope Francis. Your perceptive abilities are great, and you use them well. Many times, the people around you scratch their heads but as always, you turn out to be correct. I thank you for that my dear son.

Question: My dear Mother Mary, I'm beginning to believe that the third secret of Fatima is ever so important I should make a special booklet on this alone. This would be along with your apparition in Akita. Is this something you think would be good, appearing in another special booklet besides this one?

Answer: *Oh yes, dear son, please do that. All God's sacred children must know the truth that has been purposely hidden from them.*

Dear Mother Mary, and so it will be.

Why All the Destruction, Pain, and Agony, Dear Mother Mary

Question: dear Blessed Mother Mary: I know now for sure all the terrible agony that is going to come to God's sacred children on earth. I know now it has one singular reason. That reason is simply, the vast majority of Our Heavenly Father 's sacred children have turned their backs on the His magnificent love and instead live lives that are of Satan not of Him. So, since the majority of Our Heavenly Father 's children have rejected Him, then it is only correct and right our Father removes all of His protections regarding His sacred children's lives on earth.

I know this will bring horrific destruction, suffering, great pain, and death. In a previous answer to my question, you said no one will be spared, both the believers and unbelievers. All of this leads me to a question. Since deaths will be painful in this coming environment, will the believers suffer just like the unbelievers? Or will some consolations be made?

Answer: *Again, oh, my dearest son, your perceptions continue to amaze and delight me. You indeed are the perfect sacred child of God to be our Heavenly Father's Anointed Messenger. And the perfect person to write this book regarding my apparitions and the Godly truths that are attached to all of that. I sincerely thank you for all of this. And one day when you return to the Heavenly Kingdom you and I will have delightful times together. Discussing all these events and everything associated with your immensely hard work for our Heavenly Father to bring His truth to all His sacred children.*

With all this in mind dear son, in the back of your mind I know that what you are thinking is completely correct. Your Lord and savior Jesus Christ and my son told me what the contents of your Blessed mind is regarding this and yes you are correct. The true believers in our Holy Trinity, our Heavenly Father, your Lord and savior Jesus Christ and the Holy Spirit, which proceeds from them. All the people who believe in the teachings of my son will never experience a painful death like all the others who have rejected our Heavenly Father.

<u>*Believers Will Be Painlessly Snatched Out Of Our Physical Bodies:*</u>

When the time comes and death is very near to believers, they will all be gently snatched out of their physical bodies. And will instantly return to the loving arms of their Heavenly creator, our Heavenly Father creator of all that is seen and unseen. Briefly stated dear son, believers will not experience the pain of death rather they will experience what you experienced the time you were complaining about your lovely wife Marilyn and wanting God to heal her.

You were instantly taken out of your body to meet with two of the Heavenly elders that listened intently to what you had to say. You experienced instantaneous upward velocity that is as you put it indescribable. After a few seconds or little bit more, you found yourself within the Heavenly realm with these two Heavenly elders. Who listen to your pleas for your darling wife's life and her cure from the deadly cancer she had in her body.

These two elders remember you very well for the intensity of your love for your wife Marilyn as you now intensely love your wife, Evangeline.

I'm longwinded on this because being snatched out of your body and taken into the Heavenly realm is exactly what believers in our Heavenly Father will experience so they won't suffer any painful death. Their bodies will subsequently die or be killed by Satanic forces after their spirit bodies are gone, but by then they will be within the loving arms of their creator and our Heavenly Father. Lastly please tell people that there is nothing to fear.

<u>*For those who reject our Heavenly Father, they will die a painful death because it is of their own making.*</u>

My dearest Mother Mary, I remember that event so very well. Also, for the benefit of others I want say that right after my wife and I boarded the cruise ship I started to have this extraordinarily strong urge to go to the ship's Chapel. I knew that something significant was going to happen there. But I was so emotionally exhausted taking care of my wife and knowing that this would be her last cruise, I really didn't want any spectacular spiritual event to occur I knew would happen. Yes, I really did have knowledge of what was going to happen.

It was only until the 4th day I finally went up to the Chapel. It was a beautiful, yet, modest Chapel that was on the very highest part of the ship which I thought was so appropriate. When I arrived there was a narrow stairway that led up to the chapel. It had little cubbyholes for privacy around the perimeter of the Chapel. This is where I curled up and got comfortable and within a few minutes what you described, my dear Mother Mary, then that happened. I was gently yet at tremendous velocity, taken out of my body into the Heavenly realm where I met with two elders of the Kingdom. I complained awfully for them to save the life of my wife. After a few moments, they each looked at each other than in the blink of an eye I saw them zoom upward at a speed I could not comprehend. A moment later I was then back inside the Chapel's cubicle from where I started.

I want all of God's children that read this to realize that there is absolutely nothing that is hidden. Those within the spiritual realm know the location of everyone of God's sacred children no matter where they are and no matter what they're doing. It is like what the psalmist said, "no matter where I go, You are there."

Question: My dear Blessed Mother Mary, I know you dislike politics as I do. To me it is a pit of Vipers born out of Satanic urges. But I'm forced to consider the fact it is Satan who is working through our political system and the Satanic Vipers that have achieved political offices and power over God's sacred children in our country. So, my dear Blessed Mother, in no way do I want you to feel obligated to answer this question. A question that has naturally come into my mind and my prayers for this rapidly disintegrated country called the United States of America.

The question I have is to what extent has Satan's minions infiltrated the distinct levels of our government? Just how extensive is it at the federal, state level and our educational systems, Oh that's wrong? I already know at the county level. Especially, our schools have been thoroughly infiltrated by those who want to twist our children's minds into Satanic minions through their God-awful propaganda and destruction of moral values to our children.

I don't know how else to ask this question but, just how bad is it for those of us who are true Christian believers?

Answer: *This is a painful question to answer, my dear son. The infiltration of Satanic behavior has been going on as you have pointed out since the early 1960s. At first it was quite a minority. Of people and parents and other Godly people being busy with their own Godly lives, did not notice for many years the treachery that was slowly growing within public institutions and the public school* *system. As you like to say, it grew like a disastrous fungus promoted by people that did everything they could to hide the truth of what they were up to. I want to add dear son, that all of these people were Democrats because as you have said repeatedly, "The Democrat Party Is the Political Arm of Satan."*

As time went on the growth of Satanically oriented people in government and public education grew faster and faster. As you would put it your son it was an exponential mathematical increase over time whereas time went on it grew faster and faster. Over the last 10 years even under the presidential term of Donald Trump, the insides of government organizations and education departments kept growing like weeds.

Now, with Joe Biden as president everything has exploded, and huge vast amounts of tax money has gone to promote increasingly Satanic activity in your country. It is fair to say, now, that most school systems in the United States are controlled by Satanically oriented people. Dead set on dosing American children into the communist, socialist Satanic propaganda that destroys such things as the difference between boys and girls. Their comprehensive list of activities is Satanic and destructive.

Dear son, as you have explained many times to people, it is easy to destroy but difficult to create and rebuild. Donald Trump will be reelected later this year as the president, but the Democrats will fly into a violent frenzy as is a pure example of Satanic mind-sets. Some people will call this a civil war and that is probably correct. But this is what is to be expected from hateful Satanic oriented people. Your yet to be President Donald Trump #47 will do everything in His limited power to erase the damage done under the Satanic Biden administration.

The problem will simply be president trump will respect and follow the rules of American law while the Democrats will ignore all laws so as to regain political power against the will of American citizens.

If everybody could only read this book that you are writing, your words within here will change the course of human History for the better.

I love you so very much my dearest of sons, your Blessed Mother Mary

The Torment, Pain, and Agony to Those Who Rejected Our Loving Father

March 1, 2024

Our Blessed Mother Mary now continues telling me what it is she wants all of God's sacred children to understand. This information exceeds what was originally told to Lucia, Jacinta, and Francisco in 1917. Take heed, my dear sacred children of God.

Thank you, my dearest son, everything I have told you so far will completely unravel all man-made institutions and most all man-made infrastructure that they depend upon. Social upheaval will be beyond anything the worst that people can possibly imagine. The only thing left after this conflagration across the world will be the few remaining people who finally understand that in the end there is only God and there is only themselves.

Everything that mankind has produced will become nothing more than a distant memory. All the evil that has been built into human-made organizations, human-made buildings and bridges and infrastructure will be gone. After a time, people will be reduced to fundamentally the lifestyle of Abel, Cain, Adam, and Eve after they were expelled from the garden of Eden.

It is a remarkably interesting parallel. Such that when Adam, Eve, Abel, and Cain no longer lived in the Garden of Eden as Blessed by your Almighty Father. The sudden realization hit them as you would say like a ton of bricks. They had to scratch the ground for anything they could eat so they could survive. Yet even in that time Cain blamed anybody but himself for the results of what he did within the physical world.

This consciousness is horrifically present in all of human society today. That consciousness along with ever so many Satanically oriented people on the earth that have as their goal monstrous political power over others of God's sacred children. It is your

Heavenly Father that is in control of everything. And people who wish to contribute to God's sacred children must have in the center of their lives the attitude that they should become servants to others. To help where they can and to guide other people based on whatever knowledge they may have that is constructive and loving.

My dear son, you have said many times that the Democrat party in United States is the political arm of Satan. This is far truer than you know because <u>many of the top Democrat leaders actively engage in Satanic worship.</u> People do not know about this because it is always very secret and behind closed doors. When this book that you are writing gets published many people will throw stones at it and throw stones at you for the truth that I am telling you.

As you already know my dearest of sons, that there are high placed people in the Catholic Church that will do the same thing. They worship Satan in secret. And are using their position and power in the Church to change the holy and sacred Mass. And other Catholic prayers designed to move the Church away from its sole reason for existence which is to love and adore your Almighty Father and especially your Lord and Savior Jesus Christ.

Satan's Plan for World Conquest

It is fair to say, my dear son, that Satan over the last 60 years, as you have observed, has been successful. In penetrating the minds of so many of God's sacred children across the world. To build upon their internal desire to govern, to control, to dictate the living standards and rule of all others of God sacred children. This is so rampant throughout the entire world and manifests itself in what you call liberalism, progressivism, communism, socialism, and so on. <u>The goal is simply to put all power in the hands of very few people. So that when the Anti-Christ takes the reins of the Church which is nearby, it will be far easier to control the entire population of the world.</u> This is what is at hand, my dear son.

The End of Times Began in the 1960's.

But as I have said, this will come at a horrific price. Such that the world population will crumble into nothingness. Because of your Father removing His active support and guidance from the world. And he will let His children crumble underneath their own wretched rules and self-government that will bring only death, hardship, pain and suffering in a magnitude that is horribly unbearable to even think about.

As you have realized my dear son, all of this is now starting to happen. The prophecies of Father Pio, the information of my apparitions in Fatima as described by Father Malachi Martin and others you can see are starting to happen. As you have told your loving wife, things here will now only get worse and worse. This will be from both a societal level, a geographical level, atmospheric level and a cosmic level. There is nothing that God's sacred children can do to stop this once your loving Father withdraws His constant support for His children on earth. I know you are wondering my son how long this end of the world suffering will take. In large part it depends upon how quickly His sacred children begin to realize what the fundamental cause of all of this is.

Some will realize far quicker than others. You for example, my son realized this a number of years ago before things really started to crumble. I know you have been keeping a close eye on the activities, the Satanic activities in the Vatican. It will take quite some time for Catholics and other Christians to realize the danger that is now being constructed and posed by the Vatican toward all of the Christian believers all over the world.

I told you that when Pope Francis declared that the Anti-Christ is now on the earth, he is totally correct. The Anti-Christ has been working extremely hard behind the scenes to construct a grid of political power that stretches across the world. And that political power is Satanic from the beginning to the end, and it is he.

Pope Francis is the Anti-Christ.

The entire spiritual realm including the Heavenly Kingdom all know who and what he really is. There will be a huge schism within the Catholic Church. Where the Satanic driven people in the power structure will wage war against the people who love and cherish Almighty God and your loving Savior Jesus Christ.

Do not worry, my dear son, for this situation will not last very long. As all of this comes to fruition, along with all the geographic. The natural disasters and other calamities that will bear upon the world without the support of your Heavenly Father, Satan will see that His time is getting ever so short. It is then that God's children still left on earth will be in the greatest of danger for Satan and His demons will strike out against any person that opposes His rule over them.

My dear son, continue to accumulate emergency supplies. Food stocks that will last you in your family for quite a number of years. Especially secure clean water and do not fill up your swimming pool for that will be a wonderful store of water that will be attacked by other people who are looking for the same thing.

Speaking of things like that, my dear son, there will be roving bands of very violent criminals. Looking for anything that will help in their survival and they will instantly kill anybody who stands in their way. Ahh, my dear son, I hate so much to tell you all of this. But you are a perfect channel of distributing the future of the world. Because of all the wretched sin that continues to grow deeper and deeper not only in secular society, but also in the Church of your Lord and Savior Jesus Christ.

We, within the Trinity, know very well that you are strong, and you are indeed a fighter as your Father told you a number of months ago. You will be one of the ones that will survive all of us. And you will play a deep role in the reconstruction of the world. To bring it back to true life with the love of your Father, His only begotten son, the Holy Spirit which proceeds from them and of course, me your eternal Mother of all time. I know you have questions, dear son. Think about them and make them into a list and I will answer each and every one as you ask. I love you more than you can possibly know. Your eternal Mother Blessed Mother Mary.

April 7, 2024
None Will Be Spared, Faithful and Unfaithful

Question: my dear Blessed Mother Mary. There is one part of the third secret of Fatima that bothers me a lot and I would love to hear your comments on it. The part that bothers me is:

Answer: *"<u>Fire will fall from the sky and will wipe out a great part of humanity</u>, the good as well as the bad sparing neither priests nor faithful. The thought of the loss of so many souls is the cause of my sadness."*

Will Believer Be Treated Differently Than Those Who Continue to Reject God?

Question: I have often thought of this and like you, dear Mother, it makes me incredibly sad. My question is as people are dying from these calamities are the good and the bad both going to experience the agony and pain of death? Or somehow is our Heavenly Father going to take the faithful out of their bodies before horrific pain is experienced in the physical? I know this is spiritually possible. Because of my experience with the two Heavenly elders that took me out of my physical bodies to hear my complaints regarding my late wife Marilyn before she passed away.

Answer: *My dearest son, that is a wonderful and magnificent question. <u>Your Heavenly Father does not deal in pain for His sacred children</u>. As you know, dear son, he loves you more than you can possibly imagine. You remember the time when you were in the jet halfway across the Pacific Ocean and a beautiful golden orb appeared to you and it said to you, "God loves you." That love was so intense it brought great tears of joy to you like nothing you have ever experienced before. I know you understand that is the kind of our Father's love for all of His sacred children.*

However, those who reject your Heavenly Father will indeed experience all the pain and agony of a physical death. For they have turned their back on their Father and thus they do not possess the grace that would shield them from horrific physical pain.

For the faithful, dear love, they will not experience pain like that at all. Instead, moments before their bodies die, they will be removed from the physical world instantaneously into the loving spiritual realm. And they will be greeted by loving angels that will take care of them in every way.

Your discernment of this detail is worthy of exclamation and joy to those who continue to love Almighty God within their hearts and in their minds. Your Heavenly Father would never allow His faithful loving sacred children to feel agony and pain like what is coming to those who have rejected Him. Thank you for asking my dearest son. This is a wonderful question and I know the answer will bring relief and joy to all those who love Almighty God and me as you do.

Also, my dear son, my Son has told you that your family is protected. And they will enjoy the same sacred treatment as you do, with the one exception of your son who has rejected your Heavenly Father. But he will be given a choice. As I said before, whether he wants to continue his sinful ways and experience the consequences thereof. Or will he reverse course and come back to you, His loving Father, and His Almighty Father in Heaven.

Thank you ever so much, my dearest Blessed Mother Mary. I apologize for not getting this book out sooner than it will be because I want everybody to know your Blessed words as soon as possible.

My dear son, as my son Jesus told you, we think in the longer-term. And an extra month or so to bring this book to the marketplace is something that will not make that much difference in the longer-term of God's holy plan for His sacred children. Please do not feel bad about that there is nothing to feel bad about.

I love you.

Your Loving Blessed Mother Mary

My dear Mother Mary, some of this has already been spoken of by loving people like Father Malachi Martin and Sister Sasagawa in Akita Japan. But I must persevere to bring God's sacred children the truth what is going to befall the earth due to the increasing wretchedness and sinfulness on this earth. It is to a level that has never been seen before in the history of man since Adam and Eve.

Question: Dear Mother Mary, lately within the scientific news, astronomers have identified two very large asteroids that pass through the orbital plane of earth around the sun. This makes it very possible to collide with earth. Is the "Fire from Heaven" one or both of these asteroids, Ephosis or Beneau? Or is it multiple others we have not yet detected? I also know there are between 1.1 to 1.6 million asteroids right past the orbit of Mars.

Answer: *again, my dearest son you amaze me with your depth of knowledge in this case regarding astronomy and astrophysics. There will be multiple asteroids of very large size that will collide with the earth in the not-too-distant future. Mankind with all its rocketry technology will not be able to stop them for they are coming from a different direction than is anticipated with the two asteroids you just mentioned. They will bring death and destruction like nothing that has ever happened before on earth. They will not be as large as the asteroid that collided with the southern part of the Gulf of Mexico that wiped out 80% of all life on earth. Your heavenly Father wants to retain a large group of his sacred children. Who now thoroughly understand that they must conduct their lives in a very loving manner that is consistent with the biblical literature that was written about my son Jesus Christ.*

All modern technology will be completely wiped out and people's lifestyle will be thrown back into the equivalent of the 1800s. The time when Columbus discovered America. Life will be livable but very difficult. You can say, my dear son, that your heavenly Father hit the reset button and now life can start a new and fresh with Satan gone. All his minions have been also removed and your Lord and savior Jesus Christ will bring about a magnificent era of happiness and love on planet earth.

You will be part of the reconstruction, my dear son, however it most likely will not be in your physical form. This is something I know you will thoroughly enjoy. Creating loving societies that build new ways of living with your heavenly Father in complete control. And your Lord and savior Jesus Christ in control of all the aspects necessary to create a magnificent loving society where there will be no sin. What a lovely thought, my dear son, a large society rebuilding from the ashes that has no sin. Yes, dear son you have said this before, and it is true it will be heaven on earth.

I love you so very much, my dear eternal son. Your Blessed Mother Mary.

I know you have also uncovered the idea in your research about large meteors colliding with the earth. This will also be true as part of the torment that happens when your loving Father removes His protection. One thing that people never ever considered. Is that all the time during the development of the earth. To be suitable for the physical existence of your Father's sacred children. Way up in space, angels at your Father's bidding have always been deflecting those rocks from hitting the earth and interfering with His sacred children's development and taking what you call the earth test.

But now, your Father is removing His protection. And very large meteors will indeed assault Mother Earth like never before in the known history of your Father's children. These collisions with earth will be so great that they will also produce large tsunamis that will assault the coastlines of the major continents across the world.

The world will be reduced back to what you would call the 1800s as far as convenience, availability of food, healthcare, and other kinds of technology. All technology that has been invented in the last 100 years will vanish. As a result, there will be murderous gangs roaming the streets and the houses for anything they can take while killing the occupants. It will be a lawless time that will bring untold hardship and agony to everyone still on earth.

What we call the Christian Church or more accurately the Catholic Church will be blended into a depraved Sodom and Gomorrah-like organization that will be controlled by Satan sitting on St. Peter's throne. As I said before and you have seen in pictures, my dear love, the depraved sexual acts, and other horrendous features of fleshly exploitation will become the norm of Satanic human behavior.

Yes, my son, small children and babies will be sacrificed to Satan in rituals that I know would make you sick if I described them.

Why will a loving Almighty Father allow all of this to happen to His sacred children? The simple reason is because never before in the history of humanity has so many people turned away from your loving Father in Heaven. Each passing day it gets worse and worse with no end in sight. So, by allowing events to take their natural perverted course it will be only then that the remaining remnant, small as it will be, will then understand. Their true nature, which is fundamentally giving up to Satanic impulses and turning their backs on Almighty God. In this way the remaining people will see what life is like without Almighty God. God never will cause any of this. But rather he will simply allow things to take their natural course and people will then suffer the consequences of what they themselves have decided to do or not do.

My dear son, I know you remember raising your three children and how you handled their punishments. When you felt that they did something wrong, and you knew that they knew it was wrong but did it anyway you gave them a spanking of various intensities. After their spanking you would leave the room and wait five minutes then you would come back to your child and hug them and explain to them why they deserve the spanking they received, and you always told Him also how very much you love them. It is much the same thing, my dear son, with all of your Father's sacred children.

However, in this case your Father will simply not continue His active protection of His children on earth and let the earth do what all other heavenly bodies do within the universe. The instability of the earth will reinstate itself like it was many hundreds of thousands of years ago. The earth will no longer be a kind of Eden but rather a regular planet with no special protective features from Almighty God.

My dearest son, we should stop for now because I can see that you have become exhausted emotionally from what I have revealed to you. I would request to you, my dearest son, that we continue this sometime tomorrow. After you have had a good meal and have cleared your mind and your heart to continue listening to this most wretched secret of Fatima.

Thank you, dear Mother Mary. The emotional impact of all of this has really struck me down for now. You are correct as always and let's continue as you suggest tomorrow sometime. I do have one request which is to not let me forget anything that could be of importance. I love you dear Mother.

February 29, 2024

Dear Mother Mary, thank you so very much for a little rest before we continue on with your message to all of God's sacred children. It has been a two-day rest for me because yesterday I was not feeling up to giving you the best I have. But this morning, it is now 4 AM and I have not slept a wink, I am up and alert. So, this is a good time to continue your message to God's sacred children.

Perhaps, we can start where we left off two days ago. Talking about the absolute terrible condition the world is in. Where never before has so many people rejected our loving Almighty Father. I know that great political forces under the temptations and control of Satan who as you know has attacked me on three separate occasions and then keeps attacking me most every day of my life.

Question: With your permission, my dearest Mother Mary, should we start where we left off regarding the condition of the world?

Answer: *Yes, my dear son, good morning. I know that you did not sleep at all last night but the message I gave to Lucia Santos and Jacinta and Francisco Marto at Fatima has been on your mind constantly. Thank you for your devotion dear son. We left off* talking about the terrible disasters that are coming to the earth because of the enormous amount of God's sacred children turning their back on their loving Father. Frankly, my dear son, they have decided not to look past their own noses and see the beauty of what their Father has created for them. The awful thing is that they have become so self-centered and narcissistic. And they view life in accordance with the way they feel and not the way of your Father's rules for life, which as you know are very simple. You did a very good job in your previous book explaining the depth and simplicity of your Father's rules of existence so people will return to the Heavenly Kingdom.

My dear son, in addition to the other catastrophes I have brought forth to you, there is much more coming to the earth. As you know, my son, you are aware of cosmic cycles like the orbits of their cycles that determine and have a great influence on the general climate of the earth. Also, the earth is getting very close to switching its magnetic poles to be the opposite of what it is today. This will happen a lot sooner than people think. And will bring a lot of havoc in weather patterns and affect food supplies and so many other effects this will have on the human population will be enormous.

Earthquakes of very large magnitudes will also start to happen this year and next. These earthquakes will be not only on the continents. But also, undersea and the undersea earthquakes will be very violent. And will produce tidal waves. Which will appear as if they came out of nowhere because the people on the coastlines will not feel the earthquakes what they will see huge waves coming at them from the seas. Your Father, my dear son, has kept all of this in check in the last hundreds of years. But now rightfully so, they have decided to let the earth do what the earth does in the natural cycle of things.

My dear son, I know you understand that it breaks your Father's Heart to let these things happen. But, my dear son, even though you did not know this when you spanked your children for doing things, they know were wrong. You felt so bad that sometimes you almost cried about what you had to do to instill the proper behavior in them that they would understand not to do those things again. I love the fact, my dear son, that a few minutes after the spanking you would always without fail return to them and hug them and explain why they got spanked. And then you would tell them how much you love them.

There will also be earthquakes that are very destructive on the land as well. My dear son, you live in an area on earth that is particularly active with not only earthquakes but a few volcanoes as well north of where you are. In the beginning, these earthquakes will not bother your home. But there will come a time when your Father wants you to move away from where you are for the state that you live in is one of the worst.

They will be punished severely for this just by allowing the natural forces of the earth to reassert themselves. Speaking of earthquakes and volcanoes I know you understand about the Yellowstone National Park and the volcanic caldera there. This will come to life in the not-too-distant future. And will wreak havoc across the entire world with toxic gases and particles that will mix with the air and make it unbreathable in many areas of the world. Acid rain will fall down on the crops in the Midwest of the United States where you live. Food will become very scarce, and many people will frankly starve to death.

All of this will trigger massive social upheavals where crime will become rampant on a scale that the earth has never seen before. It is written that the living will come to envy the dead. This is a true statement, my dear son. When the time comes, your Father, your Lord and Savior Jesus Christ and I will tell you when the best time for you to move your family from the area you now live. I know you like Texas for many good reasons but depending on how things work out be open to other possibilities for the safety of yourself and your family.

On another note, dear son, I already mentioned the Milankovitch cycles that control the earth's orbit around the sun with cyclical properties that have the power to change the planet's climate. Right now, the earth is in that optimal position with regard to the cycles *but as cycles do, they continue toward less friendly positions in the cosmos. This is what is happening right now regarding the earth. These cycles are unstoppable. Your Father has been muting much of the effects of these orbital cycles and will now let the earth do what it normally would do without His protection. This will result in extremes. The people on the earth have become very much like the hardheaded Hebrews in ancient times as described in the Old Testament.*

In a very direct comparison, the manner in which your Father had to deal with them as His chosen people will now again be applied to the people on earth. To bring them to their senses and remember their real identity as you have described so well in your book, <u>God's Grand Design Of All Creation For Your Redemption.</u> Many people will say that it is the anger of God that is causing all of this destruction suffering and pain. It is not rather, as you know, my dear son, your Father is pure love. And the agony in which your Father feels because of so many of His children rejecting Him. Is such that he is only withdrawing protecting His children the natural cosmic forces that press upon the earth. This will continue until finally the few that are left will finally understand that they must return to their roots, they must return to their loving Father and His ways of behavior. It will only be then that things will turn around quickly on the earth, and it will flourish again along with all of His remaining sacred children.

March 2, 2024

My dearest Blessed Mother Mary, it has been a whirlwind of terrible emotions I have suffered with regard to the third secret of Fatima. However, my sufferings are minuscule when compared to the sufferings of so many of my brothers and sisters in Christ. So as for now they count for nothing. Over the last number of months, I have been increasingly aware of the internal disintegration regarding the Church of our Lord and Savior Jesus Christ. At first, I thought, what I was hearing was just complaining from fundamentalist Christians who never seem to be happy. But the short period of time my doubts about the veracity of their descriptions of Vatican activities, those doubts vanished.

Earlier in the sacred work of your words meant for all of God's sacred children you mentioned Pope Francis said the Anti-Christ is now on earth. You said he should know because he is the Anti-Christ. The man named Anthony Stein at <u>Return to Traditions</u> website[23] follows every detail of Vatican activities and has provided great insight into the internal demise of the Vatican hierarchy and power structure. As you know, my dearest Mother, from the beginning I did not like Cardinal Bergoglio, as he became Pope Francis. There was something about him that was very sour in my mind. Unfortunately, he has confirmed my worst fears about him.

My dear Mother Mary, I'd like to ask you to provide not only the details within the hidden third secret of Fatima, but also your personal comments on how things will progress in coming years. I thank you in advance for this, and I love you so very much, dear Mother Mary.

---

[23] Return to Tradition, Anthony Stein, YouTube

7

Third Secret of Fatima Continues

Blessed Mother Mary
March 2, 2024. 12: 07 p.m.

What was said in the third secret of Fatima regarding the Catholic Church

"Yes, my dear son, there is a lot to be said regarding your Lord and Savior's Church on earth. None of it is really incredibly good, my dear son. When I first delivered this message to Jacinta, Francisco, and Luciana in October 1917, no one would have believed what I said. It is for this reason that I asked that this part of my message not be made public until 1960. If this content were made public more than 100 years ago, everyone would have been frightened. So badly that it would have induced terrible spiritual, emotional, and even physical suffering upon those sacred children of our loving Father. So, the written words of Sister Lucia were filed away deep in the archives of the Vatican. In 1962 when Pope John XXIII read the third secret of Fatima, he decided not to release my message to the faithful. This was a bad mistake on his part for if my words were published back then, the faithful would be on guard to prevent what I said would happen. Frankly, my dear son it would have been wonderful for me to say, "God's sacred children take action within the Church to prevent what is happening now." At least it would have been delayed for a long time. Giving more time to the faithful to expand their wings and save more souls for their own sake and join their Father in the Heavenly Kingdom.

I am very dismayed that even until now anyone who has read the words of Sister Lucia are sworn to secrecy. My words were meant for

*the faithful, but the Vatican is now working against the spiritual
well-being of God's sacred children.*

Basically, what I said was quite simple, over a period of time the
hierarchy of my sons' Church would be infiltrated, would be
poisoned in all manner of speaking. The fundamental tenants of
Christianity and the will of your Father in Heaven will be
sidetracked away from the fundamental message of loving God first,
loving your neighbor as yourself and even loving your enemies. All
that is sacred and holy within the Catholic Church is being attacked,
as you write this, my dear son. By withering away piece by piece the
sacredness and the holiness of the Church that Jesus Christ has
founded for the spiritual well-being of all of God's sacred children.

My dear son, I know you have collected some pictures of the Pope
and many cardinals watching profane performances in holy places
very much like what they did in Sodom and Gomorrah. I know that
is painful for you to see, But I will ask you in this book that you are
creating that you include these kinds of pictures. So that God's
sacred children will see the truth of things and just how far the
Church has fallen away from my son and from your Almighty Father
whose love knows no bounds.

My dear son, I can perceive the tears forming in your eyes right
now and I am with you always no matter how bad you perceive things
to be. I know you can feel the presence of your Lord and Savior and
my son, I know you can feel His arm around your shoulders. This is
what will propel you to continue with delivering this kind of
information to all the faithful who need to hear this.

There are a few more things I need to say and then we will get to
the good part. Within the Church there has been so many depraved
celebrations consecrating Satan and performing Satanic acts within
the Vatican that are kept ever so secret. But they happened. I want
you to publish what was said from Father Martin's interview with
Mr. Art Bell[24]. Both our hearts are broken because of this.

---

[24] Fr. Martin Malachi's interview with Art Bell

The current pope who is the Anti-Christ will continue in his Satanic program to constantly change the holy mass to slowly erase away the true spirit of Christianity and turn it into a secular monster. At first it will be introduced as it already has as very minor changes to the laity. But then over and actually short period of time more and more changes will be done to the mass. Such that the sacredness will be erased and it will become nothing more than a secular acknowledgment of the historical Jesus and that will be it.

More and more Churches will be used for other secular purposes such as secular celebrations of things like Halloween which are innocent on the surface but are Satanic underneath the skin.

My dear son, as Christianity is slowly wiped away from the face of the earth by more and more people. Turning away from Almighty God and their own sacred nature. Christians will increasingly become persecuted in real celebrations of mass, that they will have to go underground.

Your lifelong friend, a Catholic Priest, has told you this for years. He is ever so right and has always been right in this and many other things. He has been given special graces that allows him the spiritual strength to endure a hostile spiritual environment within the Jesuit community at Santa Clara. I rejoice when you and your Catholic friend have coffee together. Be sure to give him a ride in your new car, he will enjoy that endlessly. And especially, dear son, treating him to the Alaska cruise will be one of the highlights of his life. Thank you for that.

In my previous comment, I mentioned that Christianity will be slowly wiped off the face of the earth. Except for those who were true believers in Almighty God the creator of all that is seen and unseen. As the loving Christian spirit is slowly eroded away from the hearts of people, the more and more violent interpersonal relationships will become within the public sphere and even within families. This is precisely what Satan wants. For people who succumb to these violent Satanic influences the result of their behavior will exclude them from the Heavenly Kingdom. From the very beginning, my dear son, it is the goal of Satan to destroy 100% of all of God's sacred children and his ever-increasing hatred for anything related to your Heavenly Father.

I know you remember the three separate times that Satan himself appeared to you in the middle of the night while you were sleeping. It deeply frightened you which would anybody. But over time you realized that it is Jesus Christ who is the way the truth and the life. That moment as Jesus pointed out to you when you said to yourself in the presence of your own Father that you will never treat your children the way he treated you. Confirmed the great strength you have within you. This is part of the reason that your Heavenly Father has asked you to be His Anointed Messenger. You have done wonderfully well.

Continuing on with the disintegration of our holy Church, as you know, there are now proposals circulating within the Vatican hierarchy to allow priests to be married. This will be one of the final nails in the spiritual coffin of the Church that my Son founded. For then, what makes a Catholic priest any different than normal laity? Really nothing substantial. Satan will say that this will solve many of the problems within the Church. That will be his advertisement. But his solution will bring the destruction of the spiritual identity of every Christian Catholic priest on the face of the earth. Make no mistake my dear son, your current pope will embrace this wholeheartedly and promoted until it is accepted.

The website titled, "Return to Tradition" is very good in keeping track of all the events within the Vatican and its policies. As they change and comparing this with what the true Church is all about. Add to this book, my dear son, any other topics you find appropriate from this website and Anthony Stein. The more our Christian laity knows about the internal crumbling of the Vatican, the more souls will be saved from Satanic deceptions.

Finally, my dear son, please add the other comments that Father Malachi Martin has to say about my apparition regarding the third secret of Fatima. He is a great godly man. Lastly, I will be with you always as you walk down this road of publishing what I have to say

regarding Fatima. And please put in a section regarding questions that come to your mind as I know they will. I will answer everything.
I love you my dearest son.
your Blessed Mother Mary

The Following is by Father Malachi Martin with Art Bell
May 4, 1998, [25]

The document of Fátima is not pleasant to read. It does not make sense. Unless we accept there is a wholesale phenomenon of apostasy among the clerics and laity in the Catholic Church said differently. This revelation by our Blessed Mother Mary makes no sense. Unless we accept that the institutional organization of the Roman Catholic Church throughout the world is disrupted and rendered null and void, the third secret makes no sense. Lucia said that the message from Mother Mary is for the people, and she did not want to write it down and just handed over to the Catholic hierarchy. But she did at the request of her Bishop.

Pope Pius XII received her letter and put it away at the request of Lucia and not be opened until 1960. It was opened by Pope John XXIII in February 1960, and he proceeded to say the prophecy was not true it was unreliable, and the children did not know what they were talking about. The Pope further said Lucia was only 10 years old at the time Mother Mary told her so she could not have known what she was talking about. My view on this is simply the Pope did not want people to know and was grasping for any excuse not to make public the truth of what Lucia wanted to tell God's sacred children. 10-year-olds are perfectly capable of understanding things such as this. The fact she could not yet read and write as nothing to do with it.

Pope John XXIII October 11, 1962, referred to the three children contemptuously as prophets of doom. We will have nothing to do with these prophets of doom. We are of a different age. And this

---

remains so today. Pope Paul VI also did nothing about it. Pope John, I read it and did nothing about it. Pope John II read it and also did nothing about it.

Father Malachi Martin can say nothing about it because he is under oath. Father Martin however believes that what the prophecy says is fully accurate and detailed and is certainly not the ravings of crazy children. The prophecy is a very factual statement of things.

Back then, in 1998 Father Martin was genuinely concerned about the secularization of the Church. Yes, even back then people noticed the Vatican was moving away from their very reason for existence and continues too today even more so.

What Father Malachi Martin tells us about the third secret of Fatima [26] [27]

I then said the conversation Cardinal Bea had, when the cardinal left the meeting with the Pope and his advisers reported Pope John XXIII went pale as death: "What is it, Eminence" I asked. 'Just kill a billion people. Look at this! 'He handed me a sheet of paper with 25 handwritten lines. Since that day, every word of the text remains indelibly engraved in the mind. "

Cardinal Bea made this statement about the "millions of people" because the Pope decided not to reveal the Third Secret, and to consecrate Russia. I asked Father Malaquias if I could say anything more about these "terrible" punishment that would kill a billion people. He explained that, before reading the Secret, he was asked to take an oath not to reveal. But he thought it should have been revealed, and that Our Lord and Our Lady wanted it to be known.

So, I mentioned the Third Secret whenever I could; spoke around him, giving maximum information about him, as well as the maximum number of tracks on him, without actually revealing the

---

[26]   https://www.apostoladodegarabandal.com/en/o-que-nos-conta-o-padre-malachi-martin-sobre-o-terceiro-segredo-de-fatima/

[27] https://www.youtube.com/watch?v=5CnKDjJLbvs&t=58s

text. Then, very quickly he cited a list of possible calamities and said some of them were in the Secret! Although the list included things like World War 3, the Pope's death, and the Three Days of Darkness, it was not particularly instructive. Because not all of the punishments were on the list, and not everything that was listed was part of the punishment.

Spiritual punishment the spiritual punishment apparently started shortly after 1960 resulted in the Holy Father 's refusal, Father Martin said: "Cardinals, bishops and priests are falling like leaves in hell."

"Faith disappears in several countries and continents." "Many of the elect will lose their faith .... Things will be so bad that, if Our Lady does not intervene, no one will be saved."

"God will withdraw grace" Father Malachi told me that apostasy in the Church was the background or context of the Third Secret. But he also said that this spiritual punishment was part of the punishment God would inflict if Our Lady's orders were not obeyed. In this regard, he said a disturbing thing several times: "God will withdraw Grace". This seems to be a difficult thing for God, such as sabotaging His own will "that all men be saved and come to the full knowledge of the truth." But it must be considered before a vicious circle. When the Pope refused to reveal the secret and refused to consecrate Russia, he lost the right of thanks to Himself and to the Church ..., and apparently, he was also punished for His disobedience ... " Satan will gain power in the upper echelons of the Church.

Another part of the spiritual punishment he mentioned several times was:

"Satan wants to gain power, even in the highest echelons of the Church."

The strongest statement came from a person who called Art Bell, saying an old Jesuit told him that: "The last pope will be under the control of Satan." Father Martin reported this man "would have a means of reading, or he had been given the contents of the Secret. However, he said that the quote was inaccurate. And that is because no one was authorized to quote the Secret exactly. But while the quote <u>"The last pope will be under Satan's control" is accurate,</u> <u>Father Martin changed the last two main components of that</u> <u>sentence. "The last Pope," he said, does not necessarily mean the last</u> <u>Pope before the end of time, but the last Pope "of these times."</u>

Did you mean the last pope before the Consecration of Russia? And after the words "under the control of Satan" it can have several meanings. Father Martin used to explain when talking about exorcisms and demonic activities, there are several ways in which Satan can control a human being, partially or totally. The person may have "sold the soul to the devil" in exchange for a favor, or Satan can control these people and circumstances surrounding that person .... Pope Benedict's lament to several visitors in his papal office, "my authority ends after that door! " This raises the question of how far has the Church achieved this status? We can see that spiritual punishment has been on the increase since 1960. This terrible punishment "... does not come without warning," he said. "But ... only those who have been renewed in their hearts - and will probably be a minority - will recognize Him for what he is and prepare for the tribulations that will follow. "

8

Pope Benedict
The Terrifying Revelation in
Fatima's Third Secret

Catholic Channel

This transcribes the text of the above title of a YouTube video carefully created to bring light to Mother Mary's message to all of God's children. She appeared a number of times to different children to bring her message, her warning frankly regarding the end of our world. This is more accurately stated as the end of times not the end of the earth. Great tribulations are going to be allowed by our Father in Heaven to occur on earth because he will withdraw His great protections of earth over the last many thousands of years. Our Blessed Mother Mary speaks to this in great detail and discusses also in detail what Satan has accomplished within the Church of Mother Mary's son our Lord and Savior Jesus Christ.

For years people have speculated that there is a third secret of Fatima that has never been revealed by the Church. Finally, new light has come from an unexpected place in an almost off-the-cuff manner. Released by the Vatican in the year 2000 is not complete. That something is being hidden from the public. They think it might be warnings against changes introduced by Vatican II or struggles in the Church.

When the third secret was released Mother Angelica of EWTN famously said she didn't think we got the whole thing. She said I think it is scary and that wasn't scary. Now revealed for the first time the true third secret of Fatima. It is absolutely terrifying, so terrifying Sister Lucia commanded by her bishop to write it in case something should happen to her. She spent days agonizing over it, but she could not bring herself to do it.

(**Note**: Sister Lucia is the only remaining of the three children in Fatima that received Blessed Mother Mary's complete message or warning. Jacinta and Francisco both died of a flu virus in Portugal within a few years after the apparition of Blessed Mother Mary. If Sister Lucia didn't write down the third secret, the world would never have known the warnings of our Blessed Mother Mary regarding the coming End of Times and the problems in the Catholic Church.)

In the end, after a prompt from Heaven, she did of course write it down. Exorcist Gabriel Moore said Padre Pio told him he knew the third secret of Fatima and it tormented him. Father Malachi Martin was asked to help draft a response to the secret for Pope John 23rd. He read the third secret of Fatima. Father Martin said if released, people would fill the confessionals, kneel, and strike their breasts. The new information about Fatima comes from Akita Japan. What does the apparition at Fatima have to do with Akita Japan? In 1973 our Lady appeared in Akita to Sister Sasagawa and gave her a message for humankind. The third message of Akita was given on October 13, 1973, the anniversary day of the miracle of the sun at Fatima. And like Fatima, it has been discovered recently that a part of this message from Akita was never released.

(**Note**: this really angers me. In both cases, Fatima and Akita, the Church worked to hide the truths. The truth Our Blessed Mother Mary wants to tell all of God's sacred children. Her warnings they need to know in order to avoid our Father in Heaven from removing His protections. Protections that existed on the earth, which if he does great catastrophes and millions upon millions of deaths both the good and the evil will occur. Frankly, in my humble opinion as a Christian minister and Anointed Messenger of our Heavenly Father, the Church in hiding things like this are actively doing the work of Satan himself. No, what I just said is not too harsh once you realize the gravity of God sacred children not knowing the full contents of Fatima third secret and Akita. The reason the Church did this is because these secrets document how bad the Church is and will become against God's sacred children at the hands of Satan.)

Cardinal Ratzinger the future Pope Benedict the 16th served as the head of the congregation for the doctrine of the faith at the time. In that role he studied both the secret of Fatima and the message from Akita. At one point he pronounced the two messages of Fatima and Akita are essentially the same. Bishop of Akita also said the two messages are the same. Everyone thought this was strange because the official text of the third secret of Fatima released in 2000 has nothing in common with the strikingly apocalyptic message given by our Lady of Akita.

At the end of 2023, on the Mother and refuge of the End Of Times YouTube channel, a video was posted featuring Father Elias Mary, an expert on Akita. Father Elias read a passage from Father Yasuda's book written only in Japanese. Father Yasuda served as the spiritual director for Sister Sasagawa who received the message from Blessed Mother Mary. He was considered a very holy priest having the odor of sanctity. In Father Yasuda's book we find this hidden key part of the message from our Lady given at Akita.

<u>Like the first Judas, the last pope will sell Jesus to the enemy.</u> Therefore, the era of the Anti-Christ Pope will soon come very strong. The interpreter was not Catholic, so he never really turned to the book to look at it. So, they just recently in this last visit they decided to go and look up this book (in Japanese). And they just opened it up and he put his finger, and he found the exact spot where Father Yasuda talks about the sign. The sign left by her son and Father Yasuda had this to say, the book is called, Oh Marie Zhannan. It is a holy Mother's statue and its tears, an anthology of tap recorded preachings or talks given by Father Yasuda and the book was published in 2003 in Japanese. It has never been translated into English, so he was a very important figure. He was the one as I said was like the official explainer of the message of Akita.

If sister had any confusion or didn't know what certain things meant he was the one who was supposed to enlighten her. The era of Anti-Christ Pope will soon come and so no matter how much we worry we cannot prevent this and there is nothing we can do about it. Therefore, we must properly defend our faith. The Akita and

Fatima messages are the same, meaning the Fatima message also tells us the last pope is an Anti-Christ Pope. Silenced in 1917 our Lady repeated her message in 1973. Father Elias Mary speculates about the seriousness of this part of the message to Sister Sasagawa. Had Sister Sasagawa herself revealed this she might have been punished severely, but Father Yasuda being elderly and respected no one took any action against him.

So, it may have been that the way our Lady chose to give this message. Ironically, Father Elias Mary was searching Father Yasuda's book for information on the meaning of the word *"sign left by my son."* Used by our Lady in the message when he stumbled upon the passage about the last pope as the Anti-Christ.

Finally, the third message of Akita which is the same as the third secret of Fatima can be revealed in its entirety adding the hidden sentences where they fit best. For the first time we have what is most likely the complete message as given by our Lady at Akita and Fatima.

As I told you, if men don't repent and better themselves, the Father will inflict a terrible punishment on all humanity. It will be a punishment greater than the deluge such as one will never have seen before.

Fire will fall from the sky and will wipe out a great part of humanity, the good as well as the bad sparing neither priests nor faithful. The thought of the loss of so many souls is the cause of my sadness.

If sin's increase in number and gravity there will be no longer pardon for them, terrifying, shocking. The Pope being the Anti-Christ has been set throughout the ages by enemies of the Church. What is shocking is Blessed Mary said it, so we know it to be true as she speaks truth.

Let us examine it more closely. Many times, God's revelations come gradually, but then more specifically as the event approaches. *I will put entity between the woman and the serpent.* We now know that woman is the Blessed Mother Mary of Nazareth. For example, St. Paul tells us in 2nd Thessalonians the Anti-Christ will seat himself in the temple of God. Let no one deceive you in any way! Unless the falling away comes first and the lawless one revealed, the one who opposes and exalts himself above God as an object of worship so as to seat himself in the temple of God.

In his commentary on this verse, St. Augustine wrote in City of God Book 20 is uncertain in what temple the Anti-Christ shall sit. Whether in that ruin of the temple which was built by Solomon or in the Church. There is no Vatican no Church of Rome of course at the time of St. Paul he spoke generally.

Fast-forward to 1846 our Lady appeared in La Salette France and reportedly said Rome will lose the faith and become the seat of the Anti-Christ.

This is more specific now mentioning Rome the head of the Church. One could say Our Lady's use of the words "seat of the Anti-Christ" points to the chair of St. Peter. And echoes in a more specific manner what St. Paul said about the Anti-Christ sitting in the temple of God.

Move forward again to 1917 at Fatima, Blessed Mary said, like the first Judas, the last pope will sell my son to the enemy. The era of the Anti-Christ Pope will soon come, accordingly, the one who sits on the chair of Peter will be the Anti-Christ Pope. A very specific warning since that time is near and this message is repeated at Akita Japan 56 years to the day after the miracle of the sun at Fatima.

One might object but this is the only explanation that makes sense of all we know about the third secret of Fatima. That explains all the hints and innuendos said over the last 100 years about the third secret of Fatima. It explains why Cardinal Choppy, theological advisor to five popes, euphemistically said the unreleased part of the Fatima secret predicted the great apostasy in the Church will begin at the top. It explains why Cardinal Otiviani stated to a reporter the third secret had been relegated to the bottom of the Vatican archives and that is where it deserves to stay.

It explains why Sister Lucia easily wrote of demons she saw in hell but could not write the third secret and why she confessed to being traumatized by it. It explains why Padre Pio was tormented by the third secret but not by any future catastrophic events. It explains why Father Malachi Martin said believers would fall to their knees in shock striking their breasts. It explains why Pope John XXIII nearly fainted when it was read to him.

It might explain why Archbishop Fulton Sheen said the mystical body of Anti-Christ will be set up in counterpoint to the mystical body of Christ with its Judas recruited by Satan from our church leaders. His mention of Judas might be happenstance, but it's so close to the words of Our Lady at Fatima and Akita to make one wonder. If he too read or been told the actual secret. Exorcist Gabriel Amorth said Padre Pio was tormented by only one thing. Padre Pio said to Gabriel, it is Satan who has been introduced into the bosom of the Church and within a very short time will come to rule as the ape of the Church. When told this by Amorth author José Zavala exclaimed, "oh my gosh, some sort of Anti-Christ on the Art Bell show".

A listener asked Father Malachi Martin to comment on his Jesuit priest friend telling him the last pope would be under the control of Satan. Martin's reply is yes, it sounds as if they were reading or being told the text of the third secret.

From Art Bell, most of what we know of the Anti-Christ comes from St. Paul in the second Thessalonians and from Revelation. Although, that book is replete with symbolisms so one must be very careful in its interpretation. St. Paul is clear although he doesn't say much. The Catholic catechism is also a source and we already looked at the main passage about Anti-Christ there. Interestingly Pope Benedict said the Anti-Christ does not have to be recognized as evil. He can appear acceptably benevolent, but he however goes against God. He also believed the Anti-Christ would reinterpret the words of sacred Scripture in such a way as to cause confusion. And then of course there is our Lady both that Lasalette and at Fatima with Fatima's message being repeated at Akita. From St. Paul the Anti-Christ, the lawless one, will come after the restrainer is removed from the scene. The lawless one represents the climax of human self-assertiveness against God in the temple of God itself.

Why does God allow this? St. Paul says God is sending them a deceiving power so they may believe the falsehood all those who have not believed the truth but have approved wrongdoing may be condemned. On the objection a Pope cannot be the Anti-Christ, Jesus said the gates of the netherworld shall not prevail against His Church. St. Athanasius when told the bishops were against him answered that proves they are all against the Church. Catholics who remain faithful to tradition even if they are reduced to but a handful, they are the true Church of Jesus Christ.

And Anti-Christ Pope would be a Bishop dressed in white giving the impression to the world he is the holy Father. Interestingly Jesus gave the keys to Peter making him the first Pope but a few verses later Peter contradicts Jesus and Jesus shockingly said to him "get behind me Satan," so, a Pope can become an obstacle to Jesus. He can speak like the Dragon.

This brings us back to Pope Benedict the 16th. Benedict was not a fool; he is a humble gentle learned scholarly. That was Pope Benedict a man of superior intellect, a master theologian, a man who knew the actual secret of Fatima, but he knew more. He knew of the reports of evil among the clerics both outside and especially inside the Vatican. He knew the warnings of his predecessors of the intent of God's enemies to infiltrate the Church. He could see a majority of those at the top of the Vatican holding to heresy.

He received the red report on the corruption in the Vatican. And he knew the prophecy of the popes from Garabandal namely that after John XXIII there would be four more popes, and he was that fourth Pope. And then it would be the End of Times according to our Lady at Garabandal in the 1960s. All this along with his scholarship, knowledge of theology, his privileged position in the Church hierarchy, which provided access to the secrets of Fatima, he most likely believed he was the last true Pope. And the one to follow him would be the Anti-Christ Pope as revealed by our Lady of Fatima.

Benedict reacted, he worked to synthesize Vatican II with Pratic II. He eased restrictions on the Latin mass but facing growing resistance within the Vatican and growing frail, Pope Benedict decided to act and act boldly. Knowing all that was written in Scripture must occur and what our Lady said must occur, he resigned the papacy likely believing this would usher in the Anti-Christ Pope.

Tellingly that night lightning struck St. Peters. Lucifer fell in an instant like lightning from Heaven. So, for the first time in History of the Church we had two bishops and a Pope and an honorary Pope living in the Vatican. By keeping his ties to the papacy, he retained some authority specifically regarding any teachings of heresy. If the next Pope clearly taught against Church doctrine, Benedict would speak out hoping to delay corruption of doctrine. Because of Benedict's acumen as a theologian and his title of Pope Emeritus, he could hope they would listen thus he could possibly place a check on the next Pope. Of course, Benedict knew the next Pope would most likely outlive him so why bother. Why not just live to 95 as he did shorten the years of Anti-Christ Pope. Because stress kills, he most likely would have died long before 95 had he continued to reign. In 2010 at Fatima, Benedict prayed for our Lady's triumph to come during the next seven years before the 100th anniversary of Fatima in 2017. He knew the triumph is near. By serving as a check on the lawless one he could hope to delay the full onset of the destruction of doctrinal truth in Christ's Church mitigating the suffering until our lady's triumph. Thus, he would serve as the restrainer.

From his deep faith, Benedict knew God placed him precisely at this moment in time. He alone had a vast knowledge of both Scripture and the dawning of the era of Anti-Christ. He alone was perfectly positioned to delay the full onslaught of the Anti-Christ's destruction of the Church of Jesus. So far, the first time and probably the last time the world saw two popes in white in the Vatican. One intent on serving Christ until the end and one intent on changing Christ's Church forever.

It is true Benedict never revealed the secret of Fatima or any of this for that matter? We know he knew the real secret of Fatima about the last Pope, the Anti-Christ Pope. We also know Benedict spoke in an exacting efficient manner and we now know from the American conservative in 2015 he wrote his friend a telling message.

"We see how the power of the Anti-Christ expanding and we can only pray Our Lord gives us strong shepherds who will defend His Church in this hour of need from the power of evil. He carefully chose the words this hour knowing their significance to mean now because theologically speaking the term *this hour*, may mean this moment in time or my time. So, one could argue he believed we are living in the time of the Anti-Christ.

So finally, the Fatima mystery is complete. We are living it out now at this hour as Mother Angelica suspected it is scary. Sister Lucia said the Fatima message is in the book of Revelation and the Gospels. Eschatology is the theological study concerned with the final events in the history of mankind. Our Lady used the words, last Pope, and Anti-Christ Pope. Theologically both of these happen at the end of all things as the catechism reminds us. The final trial of the Church is the supreme religious deception of the Anti-Christ. This final trial will separate the wheat from the chaff. Those who stay true to Church doctrine and those who follow the deception of the Anti-Christ who puts himself above the deposit of the faith given by God.

So, one can see how the Fatima prophecy tells us we are at the end of all things. For any who wondered what it would be like to live during the Roman persecutions or the time of the Aryan heresy, we get to live through something worse. Father Elias Mary said Father Yasuda wrote about this time no matter how much we worry we cannot prevent this. There is nothing we can do about it. We must properly defend our faith but the growth in the power of the mystery of iniquity brings us that much closer to the glorious triumph of the Immaculate Heart of Mary.

Blessed Mary promises us that in the end her Immaculate Heart will triumph. She has assured us as our Lady of the good event that when everything seems completely lost it will be her hour. The time she will act in glorious ways to restore all things. And Jesus promises he will return to slay the Anti-Christ. Our only means of help at this hour are the Holy Rosary and the sign left by my son which is the holy Eucharist and the holy sacrifice of the Mass, the Holy Eucharist. It also means confession. We need to confess, receive holy Communion often and recite the rosary daily. This is the time of the Anti-Christ, but it is also our time, we have been placed here by God at this precise moment, this final hour to look up to defend the Church.

So, when Jesus returns, He will find faith. When these signs begin to happen stand erect and raise your head because your redemption is at hand. *Be not afraid. In the world you will have trouble but take courage. I have conquered the world; behold I am coming soon!*

9

Existential Morality as Defined by Almighty God

Before I address all the wickedness that is in the world today, especially in our own country America, I need to address sinfulness or breaking our Heavenly Father's rules for us to obey. It is simpler than you think but is also harder than you think. So, this is the yardstick or the manner of measurement that will be applied to all human thoughts and actions. To decide whether or not a sacred child of God will be allowed to return to the Heavenly Kingdom from where they were created to begin with by our Heavenly Father.

Our Heavenly Father is the creator of all that is seen and unseen. He created all of His sacred children in the blink of an eye untold millions of years ago within the Heavenly Kingdom. Each of us is a sacred child of God no matter what the Satanically-minded people want you to believe about abortion and evolution where we are only piles of chemicals that happened by random circumstance.

There are only two, I repeat only two moral forces in both the physical and spiritual realms created by God. Everything is either of God or of Satan. There is nothing in between. Our Heavenly Father is pure love that is so intense and all-encompassing His sacred children cannot possibly understand it. The opposite of love is hatred. All hatred comes from Satan. Satan rules his kingdom through hate and fear. Fear is a signpost of Satan in his works on earth.

Your author of this book knows Satan personally. Satan has attacked me on three separate occasions in the middle of the night while I was sleeping next to my wife. He threatened me 50 years ago with these words, "I WILL GET YOU! I WILL GET YOU! I WILL GET YOU!" Since then, I have been forced to conduct spiritual warfare against him. He attacks me even today about three or four times each and every day. It is because I write God's truth so people like you can know our Heavenly Father and His enormous love for us all.

The God Test

If you want to know how to get to Heaven live by the following three principles of a Godly life. Like all things I write about our loving God I know for absolute certain he approves of what I say because I am His Anointed Messenger.

1. Love Almighty God above all else in your life, in creation both physical and spiritual.
2. Love your Neighbors as you love yourself. Your Neighbors are defined as everyone else other than you.
3. Love your enemies. Yes, you read that correctly.

Do you realize that if all sacred children of God on earth today lived by this trio of principles there would be no war. There would be no need for locks on doors. All security companies would go out of business. No need for police. Living by these three rules there really would be Heaven on earth. Why isn't there Heaven now? It is because of Satan in his hatred toward all of our Heavenly Father 's sacred children who are made in His image. This is you and me!

Remember all of God sacred children have two parts to them, a physical part, and a spiritual part. Our minds are really spiritual in nature and extend beyond our physical bodies. Therefore, it is our minds that are the focal point for Satanic influence and attacks. I know this personally to be 100% true. Just as a reminder this Anointed Messenger of God was attacked on three separate occasions directly by Satan himself about 45 years ago. Since then, I have been forced to conduct spiritual warfare every day of my life. Why? Satan hates me so badly because I am a writer of God's sacred truths and I do everything I can to communicate God's truth to all His sacred children which means you.

Lastly, if you love God, you have authority over Satan and you can command Satan to leave you alone in the name of our Lord and

Savior Jesus Christ. This works! I should know because I have to use it all the time.

10

Blessed Mother Mary's Closing Thoughts

Our dear Blessed Mother Mary, you and I have shared something beautiful, so sacred I feel unworthy to be involved with such magnificent wisdom you have bestowed upon all of us sacred children of God. I thank you from the bottom of my heart for everything you have said, and I hope I have not left out anything you want to be included in this book. If so just let me know and it will be included.

Question: Dear Mother Mary, please share with us your thoughts regarding your apparitions and what it is you intend to accomplish with them. I feel like because of human fear, anxiety, and other negative social pressures the sacred information you want to bestow upon God's sacred children gets cut short or not at all. I hope this book once it is published, we'll bring new light to your messages. Thank you so very much from the bottom of my heart.

Answer: *My dear favorite son, come, I have been worried about you that you have worked so very hard on everything that we have shared together. You have put yourself beyond the limits of what your body can take. And I want you to rest now at least for a little while before you finish editing and sending this book to the publisher.*

Actually, dear son, the material that exists within this magnificent book sums up to a great degree everything that I wanted to say to God's sacred children on earth. You have explained things so well that you have made it far easier for me to participate in projecting all that your Heavenly Father wants His children to know.

My Dear Blessed Mother Mary, thank you so very much for those kind loving words. I want to make this book as perfect as you are because this is your book and not mine. I am our Heavenly Father's Anointed Messenger and all the credit for things go to you that are contained within this book of Motherly love. I am looking forward one day to give you a big hug and then we can talk about all our common experiences in the creation of this work of theological truth.

I love you so very much dear Mother,

Richard

Question: Dearest Blessed Mother Mary, this has been a magnificent project of creating a book. Brings to all of God's children the actual truth of five of your most important apparitions and details about the End of Times we have entered into in the early 1960s. This has been a magnificent journey for me working with you with the love of the Trinity propelling us forward or the benefit of all of our heavenly Father's sacred children.

I would love to hear your closing thoughts on this book both you and I have created. Please, say anything you wish because whatever that is, it will magnificently benefit God's sacred children.

Answer: *My dearest son, come, when my son Jesus and I first approached you a few years ago we were very concerned that somehow, we would overwhelm you with our holy presence. And that would be enough for you not to respond to us in the way that we were hoping you would. Since those first few days you have responded to us with your entire spiritual being and intellect. You have proven beyond any shadow of a doubt that you truly are one of the most holy sacred children that I have ever encountered. I am amazed at your dedication and the scope of your knowledge. Both within the spiritual realm and the physical realm, which includes the sciences and logic and reason and an unquenchable thirst for God's truth. It has been a complete delight for me to go through everything in this book that both you and I have created for the benefit of your Father's sacred children. This has been a most wonderful experience for me, and I sincerely thank you for that.*

During the times that we spent together you always ended up overworking yourself and you got sick on a number of occasions because of your hard work and dedication. My son Jesus told me that in the previous books you have written this would be how you are. To experience this with you first hand was amazing to me. Because in all my previous apparitions and dealing with God's sacred children, while they're still on the earth, I was fighting against so much resistance. And the people I spoke with being frightened by authorities. And the Church that prevented them from saying what it is I wanted them to say to all the others of God's sacred children they come into contact with.

You on the other hand, my dear sacred child, is very fearless, and Jesus was right, you are a fighter. The best kind of fighter that you fight for the holy truth of all of creation. When Satan attacked you those 3 times when you were in your early 30s, he scared the heck out of you, but you responded so quickly coming back even stronger. Right now, while you have been writing the previous books and this one, Satan has no chance of interfering with the truth that you are the messenger of.

You have brought warmth and love to me, my dearest son, and this along with so many other qualities that you have will be remembered in all eternity. And after this book is completed, I will remain always with you. Off your right shoulder along with my son Jesus, for both of us will always have our left hands on each of your shoulders while we stand on your right side. And yes, what Jesus said is true that for your protection from Satan you now also have two very powerful angels on each side that will protect you from any spiritual and physical dangers. I thank you for everything, my dearest son. I love you ever so much for now and through all of eternity.

I love you so very much my dearest son.

Your Blessed Mother Mary

For more information contact the publisher at
info@advbooks.com

*A*dvantage
BOOKS

Longwood, Florida, USA
we bring dreams to life™
www.advbookstore.com